Counseling
International Students
Clients from Around the World

International and Cultural Psychology Series

Series Editor: **Anthony Marsella**, *University of Hawaii, Honolulu, Hawaii*

A Continuation Order Plan is available for this series. A continuation order will bring delivery of each
new volume immediately upon publication. Volumes are billed only upon actual shipment. For further
information please contact the publisher.

Counseling
International Students
Clients from Around the World

Nancy Arthur

University of Calgary
Calgary, Alberta, Canada

Kluwer Academic / Plenum Publishers
New York, Boston, Dordrecht, London, Moscow

Library of Congress Cataloging-in-Publication Data

Arthur, Nancy, 1957–
    Counseling international students: clients from around the world/by Nancy Arthur.
      p.   cm. — (International and cultural psychology)
    Includes bibliographical references and index.
    ISBN 0-306-48069-7
      1. Students, Foreign—Counseling of. 2. Counseling in higher education. 3. Cross-cultural
counseling. I. Title. II. Series.

LB2375.A78 2004
378.1'94—dc22

2003061967

ISBN 0-306-48069-7

©2004 Kluwer Academic / Plenum Publishers, New York
233 Spring Street, New York, New York 10013

http://www.kluweronline.com

10 9 8 7 6 5 4 3 2 1

A C.I.P. record for this book is available from the Library of Congress

Permissions for books published in Europe: *permissions@wkap.nl*
Permissions for books published in the United States of America:
permissions@wkap.com

Printed in the United States of America

To my daugher, Caitlin, 2 years old, and son, Travis, 1 year old.
Your arrival into our family brings job and laughter every day.
As you grow up, I hope that you will explore
the world as international students.

Preface

My first encounter with international students was in 1978 when I moved 2000 miles away from home to pursue a graduate degree program. Even though I moved within Canada, there were many new transition demands—a change in university systems, differences between undergraduate and graduate programs, a new city, and I did not know anyone in this new place. The university had advised students who were traveling to arrive a week early to prepare for classes. The residence was not open yet, so students were temporarily lodged in a dorm. It was there that I met students from many different countries, many whom had left home for the first time. The university had nothing planned for students that week and the days seemed to last forever. We decided to create our own schedule of activities and took advantage of the time to see the new city. I enjoyed getting to know students from other countries. Several cried themselves to sleep at night. I remember thinking about how hard it must be to leave family and friends behind in another country. I also remember thinking that campus services for international students need to be better planned during the first weeks in a new country. My experience working with international students was gained during 15 years of counseling and teaching at the Southern Alberta Institute of Technology, Calgary, Alberta. Students attended this post-secondary institution in existing diploma programs and in customized training programs. Students came from diverse backgrounds, including individual students who actively pursued international education, students who were sent abroad to resolve family or political issues, experienced professionals who were updating their training for specific employment positions, and groups of professionals who pursued customized training programs. It was a ritual to post the flags of the source countries and we soon filled the room with the symbols of nations joining together for international education.

Counseling international students has been full of challenges. First, I felt unprepared to address the cultural diversity in this population. Although international students face many similar adjustment concerns as local students, their situations are more complex due to living and learning across cultures. There were many times that I did not feel a strong connection in my work with clients and I wondered if they found counseling to be useful. This challenged me to deconstruct the values and methods that I had been taught in graduate counseling curriculum. It also challenged me to learn about the groups who were attending our institutions. This was a time of trial and error practices to try to make counseling more responsive to the needs of international students. When I was asked to coordinate international student services, it was timely to take a serious look at the responsiveness of the campus for hosting international students. Working with a dedicated group of student services and academic professionals helped to consolidate our approaches and expand the direction of service provision.

During the past 7 years, my professional roles have changed from counseling in post-secondary education to a faculty position as a counselor educator at the University of Calgary. In that capacity I have continued to interact with international students through instructional and research roles. As a teacher, I look forward to the exchange of learning that can occur between international and local learners in the classroom. As counseling expands professional borders and becomes more global in nature, international students are tremendous assets in counselor education programs. Perspectives can be shared and compared. It provides students with the opportunity to examine values in counseling paradigms and to exchange practices between countries. As a researcher, I am trying to gain better understanding about the strengths of international students and move a research agenda away from a focus on their problems to the coping strategies that support positive adjustment. I am also interested in how international students integrate their international experience into career development, upon the completion of their academic programs.

Many times I have heard my colleagues comment that they wished they had a guidebook for working with international students. This book was written to fill a gap in the professional counseling literature. It is the book that I wish I had access to during early years of trying to make the most of counseling international students.   The book was written to provide counselors with background information about cross-cultural transitions and culture shock to appreciate the context of issues faced by international students as they learn in a new culture. The common issues are reviewed to help counselors normalize the experience of students and to help them increase their repertoires of coping strategies.   Counseling international students inevitably involves counseling across cultures. Readers are invited to apply the multicultural counseling competencies as a framework for appreciating the unique influences of culture on both counselors and international students' experiences. In selecting the case examples for the book, I tried to select a broad range of client issues and counseling interventions.   Counseling international students requires comprehensive approaches to service delivery that extend beyond individual counseling. Counselors have a key role to play in supporting campus internationalization and in helping to improve the educational climate for international students. I hope that readers will find the book to be a useful resource for designing and delivering culturally responsive counseling services for international students.

Acknowledgements

I would like to thank the many international students that I have worked with at the Southern Alberta Institute of Technology and the University of Calgary.

We have learned together about the diverse experiences involved in crossing cultures. Completion of this book was partially funded through a standard research grant from the Social Sciences and Humanities Research Council of Canada.

Contents

1

Introduction to Counseling International Students

1.   INTERNATIONAL   STUDENTS   IN   HIGHER EDUCATION

✗ International students have a critical role in the internationalization of education. The export of education is a competitive process for attracting greater numbers of international students to educational programs in host countries and for the delivery of curriculum in "off-shore" programs. The United States leads the world in terms of the numbers of students involved in international education. Enrolment of international students in the U.S. peaked at more than 580,000 in 2001/02 and more than 154,000 American students studied abroad in 2000/01 (Chin, 2002). In Canada, enrolment of international students has fluctuated during the past 5 years, but has increased to more than 110,000 international students (Canadian Bureau of International Education (CBIE), 1999, 2002). Australia has experienced continued growth in international student numbers, with increases in enrolments both onshore and offshore. More than 188,000 international students were enrolled with Australian education providers in 2000 (Australian Education International, 2001) and those numbers currently approximate 200,000 (Bohm, Davis, Meares & Pearce, 2002). As educators consider target goals for international education, the United Kingdom provides an example where approximately 200,000 international students represent 12% of the entire student population at colleges and universities (CBIE, 1997, 2002).

There is notable growth in the numbers of international students attending educational institutions in these major destination countries. An estimated 1.8 million international students were enrolled in educational institutions around the world in 2000 (Bohm et al., 2002). The global demand for international education is unprecedented and projections indicate a long-term trend of growth with numbers expected to reach 7.2 million international students in 2025 (Bohm et al., 2002). International education is a dominant force in the export sector and is recognized as a major economic contribution to local economies. For example, it is estimated that international students contribute nearly US$11 billion to the US economy (Chin, 2002), more than

AUD$3.7 billion to the Australian economy (The Australian Government International Education Network, 2003), CAN$3.5 billion to the Canadian economy, (Association of Universities and Colleges of Canada (AUCC, 2003) and more than US $1.5 billion annually in the UK (Davis, 1997). These statistics underscore the importance role played by international students in the future of global education.

The mobility of students between countries is a core mandate of international education (Knight, 2000). International education is a relatively untapped resource to prepare students for diverse cultural and professional practices in a global economy (Arthur, 2000a, 2000b, and 2002). As the borders of trade and travel throughout the world become increasingly interdependent, students require competencies for working with people whose cultural backgrounds are different from their own. Experience as an international student provides unparalleled opportunities to develop background expertise regarding cultural and academic practices in countries around the world. Ultimately, participation in international education prepares students for future careers that involve living, learning, and working with people from other cultures (Arthur, 2000a, 2002). Recognizing the advantages of international experiences for future work in the global economy, many countries (i.e., Australia, United States, countries of the European Union) have established a goal to increase the number of their post-secondary students who study in other countries to 10% (CBIE, 1997). Likewise, higher education institutions are developing policies regarding the numbers of foreign students who are targeted for recruitment. Targets have been recommended of 5-10% of the total student enrollment (Knight, 1994). Strategic planning for the international mobility of students is important for the future of higher education. Beyond the level of individual institutions, government agencies are taking an active role in the recruitment of students from other nations. Countries such as Australia, Canada, the U.K., and the U.S. now maintain advising centers abroad for the purpose of promoting their post-secondary programs to potential international students (Davis, 1997). In order to meet targeted goals for student mobility, additional resources must be allocated for promoting international exchanges between learners from diverse countries and cultures.

The mobility of students between nations is a core component of internationalization in higher education in order to prepare learners for future roles within a global economy. This chapter provides an overview of trends within the internationalization of higher education as a context for understanding the contributions of international students. Beyond recruitment of international learners, the discussion emphasizes the importance of building campus infrastructure to support the personal and academic needs of students. Counselors have a major role in responding to the transition needs of international students as they navigate the many changes associated with living and learning across cultures. Counselors are invited to examine their multicultural counseling competencies for working with international students.

1.1 Internationalization of Higher Education

Trends in student enrolment patterns are linked to larger institutional goals to internationalize higher education. The meaning of internationalization has been debated in both the contexts of higher education and at the level of individual educational institutions (Knight, 1994, 2000). The essence of internationalization is defined as "a process that prepares the community for successful participation in an increasingly interdependent world" (Francis, 1993, p.5). An expanded definition captures the broad range of activities involved in the internationalization of higher education. "Internationalization of higher education is the process of integrating an international dimension into the teaching/learning, research and service functions of a university or college. An international dimension means a perspective, activity or service which introduces or integrates an international/intercultural/global outlook into the major functions of an institution of higher education" (Knight, 1994, p.3).

1.1.1 Values within Internationalization

A number of values are embedded in the rationale for internationalization in higher education (Aigner, Nelson, & Stimpfl, 1992; Knight, 1999; Warner, 1992). For example, international education provides opportunities for students to gain a better understanding of increasing interdependence of social and economic systems. It is also proposed that the exchange of knowledge between students of different nations ultimately promotes cooperative efforts to address global problems. Exposure to human conditions in other countries assists in the development of working alliances and social transformation for improved quality of life. A fundamental value reflected in most models of internationalization is the need to prepare students, individual institutions, and nations for competition in the global marketplace. Internationalization activities are therefore founded on values that range from humanitarian goals to values that are centered in the current business realities and commercialization of higher education (Holmes, 1996). Internationalization in higher education does not mean these values are mutually exclusive. Rather, their reciprocal influences need to be recognized and debated in institutional priorities and policies (Luk, 1997).

The growing attention paid to international students must be connected to larger social and economic changes that influence higher education. The motivation to recruit international students is inextricably linked to shrinking government resources and the need to secure alternate sources of funding in post-secondary education (Arthur, 1995). Motives for internationalization are connected to a larger context of shifting trends within the international marketplace (Knight, 2000). For example, many developed countries can no longer rely on natural resources as their primary base of economic strength. Intellectual capital is rapidly replacing natural resources as a key indicator of competitiveness. Consequently, higher education and training is rapidly emerging as one of the most competitive commodities in the international marketplace. Strategies are being developed at both national and institutional levels to ensure that educational programs are competitive in the international marketplace (Canadian Bureau for International Education, 1994/95; Johnston & Edelstein, 1993; Knight, 1999).

The commercialization of education will undoubtedly continue to be a critical and controversial direction in the future of higher education (Holmes, 1996; Knight, 1994). Although the priorities of an internationalization mandate in education have been articulated, there are also fears about the ways that international student enrolment will be managed. Tensions are evident in debates about increasing the number of international students. One point of view is that federal governments need to do more to support investments in global education. There is wide variability between countries in the amount of government funding available to position their universities competitively (AUCC, 2000). Educational institutions need financial resources for their efforts to recruit international students through funding for international scholarship and exchange programs. There is an overriding concern that the economic value of international students is driving internationalization without resources allocated to insure adequate campus infrastructure. This is coupled with concerns raised by academics about maintaining quality and standards in academic curriculum. Of further concern is that lack of preparation that academic and student support personnel receive for instructing, supervising, and advising international students (Aspland, 1999; Popadiuk & Arthur, in press). The future of education requires careful examination of the competitive marketplace for recruiting international students, indicators of success for campus internationalization (Knight, 2001), and the contributions of international students to global perspectives.

1.1.2   Contributions of International Students to Internationalization

As noted earlier in the discussion, destination countries receive enormous economic benefits from international student enrolment. The increased interest in international student recruitment is partially explained by the economic contributions they make to national economies. Although the participation of international students in higher education results in impressive economic advantages, there are innumerable advantages beyond revenue generation that deserve to be recognized. "While there is a great deal of interest in attracting international students to ... institutions ..., it is a common belief that their potential as catalysts and agents for internationalization has not been fully realized" (Knight, 1994, p. 7). The value of international education is more than an economic resource. Apart from the economic benefits that international students bring to post-secondary institutions, there are countless tangible and intangible benefits for supporting the cross-cultural exchange of knowledge between learners from many cultures (Dei, 1992; Diambomba, 1993; Knight, 2000; Lambert, 1992; Wilson, 1991). International students facilitate internationalization in the following ways (Francis, 1993):

- Developing networks for worldwide contact;
- Providing resources to internationalize educational curriculum;
- Developing business connections across cultures;
- Negotiating linkages and reciprocal exchanges between international institutions;
- Generating revenue through internationalization to benefit other departments and members of an educational institution;
- Developing linkages in the local community for economic and cultural benefits; and,
- Establishing long-term international relations.

International students in higher education provide cultural and economic benefits that can have both immediate and far-reaching effects. Upon returning to their home countries, international students represent their experience of living and learning in the foreign country and in the host community. This group of alumni are powerful ambassadors to promote further student exchanges and to forage new international project partnerships (Diambomba, 1993; Francis, 1993).

1.2 The Response of Educational Institutions

Unfortunately, the financial restraints faced by post-secondary institutions have impacted foreign student recruitment and admission practices. As fewer institutions are willing to subsidize foreign students, particularly undergraduates, recruitment efforts are directed towards those students who can finance the full costs of their foreign education out of personal resources. Many institutions are expanding programs beyond their traditional academic curriculum to offer customized curriculum for the specific training needs of people from other countries. Along with global education initiatives, these initiatives are partly in response to the demands to secure external funding sources. The recruitment of international students is now a critical base of institutional funding in higher education.

In a competitive educational marketplace, the reputation of educational institutions lies in their capacity to deliver quality academic and support services. The danger lies in treating international students as "commodities" (Magnusson, 1997) without considering their roles in a rich cultural exchange and how their learning experiences need to be supported. In conjunction with increased recruitment efforts, campus internationalization programs are needed to support the enrollment of international students (Cunningham, 1991; Francis, 1993; Knight, 1994; Tillman, 1990). In response to the growing involvement in international education, institutions are examining ways to build infrastructure that fosters meaningful academic and support programs for international learners. A key feature of campus internationalization includes the preparation of campus personnel to gain the competencies to support international education initiatives. This involves preparing the campus community, including faculty, staff, and other students to develop new skills, attitudes, and knowledge to support international activities (Knight, 1994). Cross-cultural competencies have been emphasized to assist the campus community to make the transition from traditional educational paradigms to embedding international perspectives in daily campus operations. The emphasis on the human dimension of internationalization programs is to adapt a way of thinking and behaving that is summarized by the axiom, "Think globally; Act locally!"

1.3   Creating a Supportive Campus Environment

As part of internationalization programming, personnel need training to work effectively with international learners. It is highly presumptuous to expect faculty, staff, and other students to effectively interact with international students without adequate resources and training. Otherwise, campus personnel are left to rely on their previous experience with local students to guide their interactions with international students. The risk is that prior experience based on a specific cultural context may be inappropriate or detrimental for learners from other countries. Even with good intentions and an interest in students from other nations, lack of preparation to work effectively with international students can result in frustrating, unproductive and even harmful interactions. Risks increase for dissatisfaction by both international students who attend foreign institutions and the people who come into contact with them. Consequently, internationalization programs and services must be responsive to the needs of both international students and the campus personnel who interact with them. Ultimately, success in international educational markets is linked to the satisfaction of student consumers. International education is highly dependent upon the degree to which campus personnel are prepared for learners from other countries.

A supportive campus environment is essential for assisting international students to attain their academic and personal goals of studying in a foreign culture (Tillman, 1990). International students have unique issues that require staff to understand the ways in which culture impacts living and studying abroad. Both academic and student services staff must consider how their roles contribute to the learning process through effective cross-cultural relationships. Campus personnel must be aware of the complications of learning in a second language, common transition issues, and ways to assist international students to feel at ease about accessing services. There is a need for a campus network of resource people who have demonstrated cross-cultural sensitivity and interest in international students. The important point here is for educators to realize that many issues impact the academic success of international students. It is insufficient that campus personnel be summoned to embrace an internationalization mandate that includes international students. Administrators of post-secondary schools have leadership responsibilities for funding campus programs and resources designed to support international students (Cunningham, 1991; Francis, 1993).

The value of international student enrollment is seldom questioned. However, what must not be lost sight of is the importance of quality assurance in the educational experiences offered to international learners. A serious question needs to be examined: "Are we doing a good job of integrating international students on our campuses and in our communities, or are we simply enrolling them and then leaving them to cope on their own? (Cunningham, 1991). Along with access to quality academic programs, quality in service provision of campus support programming is also a priority. Campus support services are fundamental resources for assisting students in ways that impact their academic. Beyond recruiting international students, there is an ethical responsibility to provide programs and services that support both their academic and personal success (Arthur, 1997). Institutions have responsibilities for meeting the needs of international students through the following ways (Cunningham, 1991):

1) Providing international students with accurate information and ongoing support while residing in the host country in ways that considers their special status as international students;

2) Facilitating interactions and development of relationships between international and local students, as well as supporting

relationships between the diverse nationalities of international students;

3) Supporting the development of relationships between international students and members of the local community; and,

4) Encouraging international students to have a voice in expressing their needs and in organizing as a group to form effective working relationships with campus personnel and representatives of the local community.

Campus internationalization programs require a comprehensive approach to hosting international learners.

1.4   The Importance of Culturally Responsive Counseling Services

The transition experiences of international students make student counseling an essential campus service. Counselors have a key role in helping international students to cope with the transition from their home country and loss of support systems, to build local networks that support academic achievement, and to prepare for the transition home. As members of a student services division, counselors are frequently called upon to directly assist international students, or to intervene on their behalf with other members of the campus community. However, depending upon the availability of services in their home countries, many international students are unfamiliar with the nature of counseling and how services may support their academic goals. Internal barriers based on the perceptions of international students and external barriers existing on campus may be prohibitive for students to access counseling services.   Several challenges pertaining to access must be overcome in order for counseling to be responsive to the needs of international students.

International students have unique issues that require an understanding of the ways in which culture impacts the experience of living and studying abroad. Without adequate preparation of counselors, there is a greater risk of perpetuating problems of early termination, client dissatisfaction, and a sense of isolation experienced by international students (Anderson & Myer, 1985; Pedersen, 1991).   Concurrently, without preparation for working with international students, counselors may be frustrated about their efforts to understand and address client issues that are compounded by complex cultural factors.   Counselors are challenged to consider how their values, counseling styles, and delivery methods accommodate the needs of international students and to increase their multicultural counseling competencies for working with this diverse group of students.

Counselors need to consider how cultural values and assumptions impact the academic and personal experiences of international students. Without an awareness of the influence of culture on the education process, there are dangers of stereotyping and cultural misunderstandings that can exacerbate student difficulties. International students have reported problems of discrimination and racism, primarily stemming from academic curriculum and interactions with other students and staff (Dei, 1992). World events and media coverage are influential in perpetuating negative stereotypes about students from particular countries. Following the tragic events of September 11, 2001 in the United States, the public was bombarded with media images of the "face of terrorism." Students from Arabic nations, and particularly those of the Islamic faith were suddenly scrutinized in ways that would not have otherwise occurred. Policies of admission and tracking functions were reviewed (Greenberg, 2003) and debates have been held concerning the source countries of international students, security issues, and debate about which academic programs should be open for enrolment (North, 2002). Groups of international students can feel isolated and separated from a sense of community because of strong public perceptions. Personnel who work with international students are not immune to biases about international students, including the superiority of one cultural group over another. The socialization process exposes people to cultural beliefs about world events and relations with specific nations. It is important for counseling staff to consider how their personal views impact their professional roles with international students.

With the recent attention paid to multicultural issues in counselor training programs, there is, arguably, information and training available for counselors about working with clients from other cultures (Sue, Ivey, & Pedersen, 1996). However, counselor education programs rarely include information about international students. General attention to multicultural issues falls short of equipping counselors to effectively assist international students (Arthur, 1997; Jacob & Greggo, 2001). Counselors may unintentionally impose ethnocentric biases into their work with this student population. As illustrated in the following examples of myths about international students, there are many misconceptions and misunderstandings that, unfortunately, continue to marginalize students from other countries. Counselors who read this book are invited to learn more about international students and to learn about ways of developing culturally responsive services.

1.5   Myths   and   Misconceptions   about   International Students

Misunderstandings and misconceptions are perpetuated through lack of information about the realities of students who choose to live and learn in another country. Unfortunately, biases in the counseling literature contribute to a negative view of international students as "problem laden" and "difficult clients". This focus on problems, with few suggestions in the literature for counselors about *how* to work with international students poses one of the biggest barriers in organizing culturally responsive counseling services. Counselors can begin to increase their competencies through addressing some of the common myths associated with international students.

1.5.1   Myth #1: Local Students and Members of the Host Community Subsidize International Students

The tuition fees for international students are typically two to four times higher than tuition fees paid by local students. Many people in the local community, including students and parents, do not realize that education is subsidized through their provincial and federal governments. Local students pay directly only a portion of their total tuition costs. International students do not receive this benefit. International students are often aware that they are attending classes together with local students, receiving the same education with notable cost differences.

1.5.2   Myth #2: Foreign Students Take "Seats" in Educational Programs Away from Local Students

There is not a competition between local and international students for space in educational programs. Institutions establish the number of seats available in academic programs as part of base funding paid to their educational institutions by government funding. International students are usually accepted as "extra to program" quotas. However, growing competition for admission to higher education and space restrictions in overcrowded campuses are likely to perpetuate a sense of competition between student groups about who "deserves" to be enrolled.

1.5.3 Myth #3: International Students Are the "Cream of the Crop" from Their Country

This statement implies that all international students are the top academic achievers from their country. Due to their excellent record of achievement, some international students are awarded sponsorship for foreign education by their home governments or through competition for international education exchanges within the host country. In these cases, international students represent the best and the brightest learners from their country. However, no prior assumptions about academic abilities should be made. There is wide variation in the background preparation of international students. This is partially accounted for by differences in educational curriculum between countries as well as the individual motivation and accomplishments of students. People become international students for a variety of reasons, and academic achievement is only one of the reasons that individuals choose to study in another country. Counselors must also guard against assuming that international students are in a "deficit" position in terms of academic achievement. Depending upon prior academic preparation, some international students may find the standards of the host academic institution to be below those of their home country.

1.5.4 Myth #4: Any Student Can Become an International Student

Becoming an international student requires satisfying immigration requirements and securing temporary visas for educational purposes. Immigration authorization must be approved from the home country as well as meeting the requirements of immigration authorities in the host country. Conditions in their home country prohibit many individuals from pursuing foreign education. Immigration relationships between countries are also a mitigating factor. Beyond immigration issues, the costs of a foreign education mean that opportunities for students are not equitably distributed. Students from poor families in many countries considered to be "developing nations" may not be able to afford the same educational opportunities as students from wealthier nations.

1.5.5 Myth #5: International Students Come from Wealthy Families

The discussion raised in the previous point should not leave the impression that all international students come from wealthy families. Access to financial resources is a critical factor to pursue a foreign education. Some families pool resources to provide an educational advantage for one family member. In addition to private funding, some students receive sponsorship through their governments, employers, or international development programs. Even within groups of students who travel together in sponsored educational programs, there can be wide disparities in the financial resources available to individual students.

1.5.6   Myth #6: Previous Travel Experience Prevents International Students from Experiencing Culture Shock

Many international students underestimate the degree of culture shock they will experience. As a general rule, the greater the contrast between the individual's home culture and the host culture, the greater the severity of a culture shock reaction. Prior experience helps individuals to anticipate change, but novel features of a new cultural environment may prompt a reaction of cultural shock. This is difficult for individuals who do not expect adjustment difficulties and who perceive themselves to be competent in meeting the demands of a new culture. International students are often unprepared for the transition home, in which changes in the home environment or internal changes in themselves prompt reverse culture shock. Education about culture shock helps international students to normalize their experiences and to develop effective coping strategies.

1.5.7   Myth #7: International Students Do Not Use Counseling Services

The usage rates of international students, in comparison to local students, have been debated in the counseling literature. Some sources indicate that international students typically access counseling for only a single session. Usage rates may be reflective of a number of factors including international students' knowledge about counseling services, their experiences with a counselor, and the degree to which counselors are engaged in outreach services on campus. The pressing need to resolve transition demands may be reflected in the problem-focused agendas of students who seek counseling services for practical solutions. Like all clients, international students prefer counseling that is meaningful to them. The extent to which international students utilize counseling services depends upon them receiving culturally responsive services that meet to their needs.

1.5.8 Myth #8: International Students Are Difficult Clients to Work With in Counseling

It is important for counselors to realize that counseling services is a foreign method of helping from the point of view of many international students. Counselors need to take extra steps to help international students understand what counseling is, how it is relevant to their academic and personal adjustment, and how counseling interventions can support their success. Cultural views of help seeking must be addressed in order to promote motivation for additional counseling sessions. When international students are difficult clients to work with, this is usually a sign of cultural impediments to an effective working alliance. Counselors can increase their competency levels and comfort levels for working with international students through becoming familiar with common issues, gaining knowledge about the cultures of students, and through enhancing their skills for counseling clients from around the world.

1.6 Overview of the Book Chapters

This book was written specifically to introduce counselors who work in school settings to the issues faced by international students during the transition to living and learning in another country. In describing the student population that studies in other countries, the term foreign student and international student have both been used. There have been objections raised against the use of the term foreign student due to a negative or pejorative connotation, although others consider foreign a positive or exciting adjective (Holmes, 1996; Pedersen, 1991). For the purpose of this book, the terms are used interchangeably but the term international student is preferred.

The chapters in this book address the role of counseling in providing campus support services to international learners. Beyond the theoretical and research sources that inform the discussion, the focus of the book is on offering practical suggestions for counseling international students. The book has been developed from sources of counseling literature and from the personal experiences of the author in counseling and instructing international students. It was written with the intent of encouraging counselors to become involved with international students on their campuses and to enjoy the many rewards of working with clients from around the world.

Chapter 2 introduces counselors to the psychology of cross-cultural transition. A defining characteristic of international students is that they are learners in cross-cultural transition. Counselors need to be familiar with models of transition as an organizing framework from which to appreciate the experiences of international students. Many of the problems that international students face are connected to their experience of culture shock. Popular models of culture shock are reviewed in Chapter 2, including some of the limitations of these models. Counselors are encouraged to supplement their understanding of culture shock through knowledge about the processes of acculturation and cultural learning.

Chapter 3 provides an overview of the common transition issues faced by international students in their adjustment to living and learning in another country. The discussion emphasizes the importance of academic success for international students. However the academic and personal achievement of international students is often closely connected to demands in other domains, including financial resources, language competency, and developing social support in the local environment. The discussion in this chapter provides an overview of the common issues faced by international students while reminding counselors that the individual experiences of international students are unique.

Chapter 4 is devoted to the cross-cultural transition of re-entry. More attention has been paid to the initial stage of entering a new culture and the common issues of adjustment. However, another defining characteristic of international students is that they are temporary sojourners in the host culture. Leaving the host culture and returning home is another stage of cross-cultural transition. Many international students do not anticipate that returning home will prompt a reaction of culture shock. Returning home to a familiar culture may be disrupted through changes that have occurred at home while students have lived in another country. For many students, it is the degree of internal change that leads them to experience culture shock during the transition home. In this chapter, suggestions are given for counselors to assist international students to integrate their international experience and to prepare for the re-entry transition.

Chapter 5 introduces counselors to multicultural counseling competencies for working with international students. Counselors are encouraged to examine the concept of cultural encapsulation and its potentially harmful influences on professional practice. Multicultural counseling competencies in four domains are described in this chapter, including self-awareness, knowledge, skills and organizational development. Examples are provided of ways that counselors can apply multicultural counseling competencies with international students. This requires counselors to examine the scope and function of counseling services. Apart from the traditional counseling domains of individual and group counseling, counselors are challenged to expand their roles to include campus outreach, consultancy, psychoeducational programming, and advocacy. This chapter is designed to help counselors develop a systematic approach in the delivery of counseling services with international students.

Chapter 6 provides seven case examples of counseling international students. These examples were selected from the author's personal experience of working with international students. Each scenario provides a central issue; however, the cases were chosen to illustrate how several transition issues can overlap in the presenting concerns of international students. In reading this chapter, counselors are invited to define the presenting issues, to examine the cultural complexities in each case, and to select options for counseling interventions. The case examples illustrate the multiple roles that counselors can adopt in providing culturally responsive counseling services to international students.

Chapter 7 is devoted to specific areas of professional practice in working with international students. This chapter is divided into seven sections organized to help counselors better understand the issues of international students and how to enhance multicultural counseling practices. Some of the topics reviewed in this chapter include counseling styles, views of the counselor, cultural attitudes towards help-seeking, ways to increase access to counseling services, cultural inquiry in counseling, group approaches and suggestions for delivering workshops, language proficiency in counseling, and the counseling role of cultural therapist. Suggestions for future directions in counseling international students are also discussed. This final chapter is packed full of practical tips for enhancing counseling practices with international students from around the world.

2

International Students: Learners in Transition

2. THE PSYCHOLOGY OF CROSS-CULTURAL TRANSITION

International students are differentiated from other populations who work and live in other cultures due to their unique status as temporary sojourners in a foreign country (Martin & Harrell, 1996). The transition between home and host cultures involves a period of adjustment generally described as culture shock (Oberg, 1960; Ward, Bochner, & Furnham, 2001). Major differences in the educational and social customs between a student's country of origin, and the host culture compounds adjustment (Pedersen, 1991). Culture shock results from external changes and differences in the physical environment, e.g., climate, food, transportation, and internal changes such as role differentiation and status loss (Pedersen, 1991). During cross-cultural transition, familiar roles, traditional sources of self-validation and means through which social support is communicated are disrupted (Ishiyama, 1995a, 1995b). Role changes and loss of status in the new culture can have a profound impact on the sense of security felt about one's personal identity. Crossing cultures may mean shedding prior roles, usual ways of operating in those roles and building new sources of personal identity. There are immediate demands for learning new ways of behaving in the new culture in order to meet role expectations. International students' capacity for role learning is an important influence on their adjustment (Pedersen, 1991). Along with role changes, if sources of support or other coping strategies are inadequate, international students may experience debilitating stress associated with the adjustment to life in the new culture (Mallinckrodt & Leong, 1992; Wan, Chapman, & Biggs, 1992). Thus, an understanding of the relationship between stress and coping can be helpful for appreciating individual differences in way that cross-cultural transitions are managed (Chen, 1999; Lazarus, 1997; Lazarus & Folkman, 1984; Ryan & Twibell, 2000).

The majority of research about international students has emphasized adjustment problems, paid less attention to the factors that lead to successful outcomes, and has generally ignored the dynamics involved in cross-cultural adjustment (Church, 1982; Pedersen, 1991). Familiarity with theoretical perspectives of cross-cultural transition provides counselors with frameworks for understanding the adjustment issues faced by international students. This chapter expands upon theoretical approaches used to describe the process of cross-cultural transition. Models of culture shock are outlined to provide background information about stages of adjustment within cross-cultural transition. Contributions from the literature on acculturation, stress, and coping are included to broaden theoretical perspectives on cross-cultural transition. A recurring theme throughout the discussion is that crossing cultures involves challenges to personal identity and ways of understanding the surrounding world. Assisting international students to manage cross-cultural transition requires understanding about the disruptions they face and the ways that cultural learning supports positive psychological adjustment.

2.1   Defining Cross-Cultural Transition

Transitions involve a process in which individuals experience a shift in their personal assumptions or worldview (Schlossberg, 1984, 1992). Transitions often entail loss as familiar ways of operating, routines, beliefs, or settings must be left behind in order to adapt to changing life circumstances (Bridges, 1991). During cross-cultural transitions, it is exposure to norms and behavior that contrast one's own culture that poses challenges for an individual's understanding of self, assumptions about others, or the beliefs about the world (Ishiyama, 1995a, 1995b; Zaharna, 1989). Concerns about personal identity are heightened (Berry, 1997; Martin & Harrell, 1996). During transitions, people require effective coping resources for managing perceived demands (Schlossberg, 1984, 1992). Taxonomies of coping skills have been developed to prepare people for a variety of life transitions (Brammer & Abrego, 1981, 1992; Lazarus & Folkman, 1984) including cross-cultural transitions (Arthur, 2000b, 2002; Winkelmann, 1994).

People in cross-cultural transition are immediately immersed into situations that require learning and adjustment to new role demands. Disruptions to familiar ways of interacting and usual sources of personal validation, along with the need for rapid acquisition of culturally appropriate responses, lead to the sense of confusion and conflict associated with culture shock (Ishiyama, 1995a, 1995b; Winkelman, 1994). The original models of culture shock (Lysgaard, 1955; Oberg, 1960) alerted us to the shifting nature of cross-cultural transitions and people's reactions over time.

2.2   Culture Shock and Cross-Cultural Transition

Early studies described culture shock as a stage model that resembled a U-curve in terms of people's pattern of adjustment (Lysgaard, 1955). Three stages of culture shock were described as contact with the host culture, conflict with the host culture, and adaptation to the host culture. The predicted pattern suggests progression from the initial excitement and optimism about entering the new culture to a downward shift in morale, which reflect cross-cultural difficulties and accompanying negative affect. In the third stage of adaptation and recovery, there is a shift towards the top of the U-curve as strategies for managing in the host culture are mastered and morale improves. A W-curve model was proposed as an expansion of the theoretical tenets of culture shock (Gullahorn & Gullahorn, 1963). This revised model takes into consideration an additional stage of adjustment when people return to their home culture.

2.2.1   Limitations of Early Models of Culture Shock

The contributions of the classic models of culture shock (e.g., Gullahorn & Gullahorn, 1963, Oberg, 1960) are that they have alerted us to the fact that people's adjustment to cross-cultural transition shifts over time (see Figure 1). These models have heuristic value for framing the changes and reactions experienced by international students (Crano & Crano, 1993; Parr, Bradley, & Bingi, 1992).

The course of adjustment proposed in models of culture shock has been debated and research has found contradictory evidence (Church, 1982; Furnham & Bochner, 1986). These models have also been criticized for the lack of attention paid to individual differences, including important intrapersonal and interpersonal variables that impact adjustment in crossing cultures (Furnham & Bochner, 1986; Ward et al., 2001). For example, the U-curve and W-curve models of culture shock do not consider the entering behavior and personal adjustment at the time of moving to a new culture. Experiences in the new culture may also have different meanings and valence of personal importance over time. There are many important interpersonal dynamics that impact adjustment, e.g., relationships with instructors and other students, efforts to make new friends, racism and discrimination. In order to understand international students' experiences of cross-cultural transition, both personal and environmental factors must be taken into account (Furham & Bochner, 1986; Ward et al., 2001).

One of the most serious limitations of the classic models of culture shock is the generalization about people's experience in cross-cultural transition. Research has indicated that there is substantial variation between individuals and groups in their cross-cultural experiences (Berry, Kim, Mindle, & Mok, 1987; Ward & Kennedy, 1993). Research with other populations in cross-cultural transition, i.e., workers on international assignments, has emphasized the multidimensional nature of cross-cultural

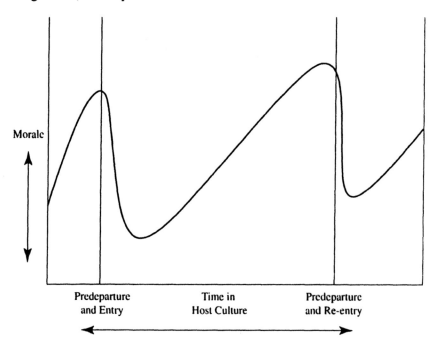

Predeparture   Time in   Predeparture
and Entry   Host Culture   and Re-entry

Figure 1. Illustration of the W-curve model of adjustment.
    Note. This illustration is adapted from Gullahorn and Gullahorn (1963) to show a general pattern of adjustment. Many international students' experiences vary from this W-curve model. Shifts in morale occur as students gain mastery over specific aspects of cross-cultural transition

adjustment, including factors such as the individual's background, circumstances that lead to the cross-cultural transition, and contextual factors such as the cultural novelty of the host country (Berry, 1997; Parker & McEvoy, 1993). In accounting for individual differences, it is important to consider that people's perceptions of aspects of the new culture that are stressful shift over time. Therefore, in order to understand the experiences of international students in cross-cultural transition, it is important to consider the specific aspects of the new culture that they experience as stressful (Chen,

1999; Ryan & Twibell, 2000). Their coping efforts in different stages of cross-cultural transition must be assessed in order to identify the strategies that lead to either positive or negative adjustment (Lazarus, 1997; Searle & Ward, 1990, Walton, 1990; Williams & Berry).

2.2.2   Culture Shock Revisited

Recent conceptualization of culture shock (Pedersen, 1995a; Ward et al., 2001; Winkelman, 1994) overcomes many of the criticisms levied against earlier models. Rather than viewing stages of culture shock as discrete, they are considered to be sequential and cyclical. Four primary phases of culture shock portray the general experience of cross-cultural transition: 1) the honeymoon or tourist phase, 2) the crisis or disintegration phase, 3) the reintegration and gradual recovery phase, and 4) the adaptation or resolution phase (Pedersen, 1995a; Winkelman, 1994). The processes within each phase account for the shifting nature of people's experiences in cross-cultural transition and that adaptation occurs through many different patterns. As people encounter new demands that require additional adjustment, there can be movement between the stages. It would appear theoretically possible for people to be in different stages of culture shock, depending upon what specific aspects of culture they were attempting to manage. Recent conceptualization of culture shock allows counselors to simultaneously consider the general stages of adjustment and the specific issues of crisis and adaptation that change during cross-cultural transition. The general stages of a model of culture shock will be elaborated on, supplementing the discussion with additional perspectives on cross-cultural transition and the experiences of international students.

2.2.2.1   Honeymoon or Tourist Phase

The first stage of the cross-cultural transition is typically characterized as the *honeymoon or tourist phase* (Pedersen, 1995a; Winkelman, 1994). It is assumed here that people who enter other cultures have positive expectations, and look forward to their experience. In this initial state there is usually a fascination with cultural differences and contrasts are appraised as exciting and interesting. Although there may be feelings of stress associated with the cross-cultural transition, they are usually viewed in positive ways, somewhat opposite to the undesirable aspects of culture shock.

However, certain qualifiers about this depiction of cross-cultural transition are in order. To begin with, cross-cultural transitions vary according to dimensions such as the degree of voluntariness, mobility and permanence

(Berry, 1997). For example, the majority of international students voluntarily decide to study in another country in order to expand their educational and career opportunities. For other international students, cross-cultural transition is not entirely voluntary and more of a reaction to undesirable or unwanted circumstances in their home country. Mobility to another country and the accompanying cross-cultural transition may be "voluntary" but not the preferred choice. Pre-departure circumstances may lead to students feeling conflicted about leaving the home culture and influence their expectations about entering the new culture. A second qualifier pertains to the temporary status of international students in the new culture. It is a condition of immigration status that international students are permitted to live and study in a foreign country for a restricted period of time. Their temporary status may mean that international students do not have the same level of commitment to the new culture as people who are making a permanent transition. Yet exposure to a new culture brings the international students face to face with other people who do not share a common basis of cultural values. This contrasts the experiences of other people whose cross-cultural entry is relatively sheltered and structured, i.e., vacationers, pre-planned business, and therefore may have very little exposure to the daily realities of managing in a foreign culture (Winkelman, 1994). Although there may be similarities in the initial positive expectancies of crossing cultures by international students, the personal isolation and need to quickly immerse into the local culture make this initial stage short-lived.

2.2.2.2 Crisis or Disintegration Phase

The ending of the first stage of culture shock and the transition into the *crisis phase* depends upon a number of factors pertaining to the individual, the amount of preparation, and factors in the new cultural environment (Furnham & Bochner, 1986; Winkelmann, 1994). People may experience crisis almost immediately upon arrival to the new culture or this reaction may emerge after several months. Though timing varies and there is a broad range of individual reactions, the essence of crisis is dissatisfaction with the host culture. Aspects of cultural difference that were fascinating initially are later perceived as sources of irritation and disappointment. In extreme cases, individuals reject the local culture and cope by erecting barriers to viewing any aspect of the local surroundings as rewarding. This shift in thinking about the local culture is accompanied by strong feelings such as lack of control, depression, anxiety or physiological reactions of stress. In this phase, individuals polarize their thinking about home and host cultures and may establish a firmer commitment to culture of origin. What is particularly difficult for people in this stage of culture shock is the preoccupation and longing to return home.

During the transition to the host environment, international students are faced with contrasts regarding their own culture. Exposure to new ways of living can be the source of considerable dissonance. The discomfort between prior ways of knowing the world and new cultural norms may pose challenges for international students' personal and cultural identity development (Sue et al., 1998). Students vacillate between acceptance and rejection of features of both the home and host cultures. For example, on some highly visible dimensions such as clothing, students may "overshoot" and become more like the host culture. On other variables that are less clearly linked to behavior, there can be a type of "ethnic affirmation" regarding commitment to one's original cultural beliefs (Triandis, 1991).

International students may vacillate between various ways of managing their identity during contact with the host culture (Berry, 1985, 1997). For some students, cross-cultural dissonance results in a firm grasp on home values and rejection of the host culture. Counselors need to be aware of the conflicts that occur as international students face values issues that may be either normal developmental issues, i.e., living away from parental control, or those accentuated by exposure to new and/or competing values in the new culture (Pedersen, 1991).

When students enter into a stage of crisis and it extends over a prolonged period of time, the risk is that students remain closed to experiencing specific aspects of the host culture that they might otherwise enjoy. The prognosis for a prolonged stage of crisis is the risk of problems escalating in the host culture, e.g., falling behind on academic responsibilities, serious health concerns. When students question their decision to remain in the host culture, a decision to leave must be weighed very carefully. Returning home prematurely can have serious consequences for an individual student or for those who have supported the individual (Harrison, Chadwick & Scales, 1996; Wehrly, 1988). It may be difficult to resolve the sense of personal failure that accompanies early termination of a cross-cultural experience.

2.2.2.3 Reorientation and Re-Integration Phase

Not all crises lead to aversive resolutions. Most people in cross-cultural transition learn how to adjust effectively. Through cultural learning and trying out coping strategies, international students become reoriented in the host culture (Pedersen, 1995a; Winkelman, 1994). This may occur through trial and error practices or through interventions designed to address transition demands.

Some international students cope by limiting their interaction in the host culture and associating with other students from a similar cultural background. This can reduce the isolation and sense of frustration often experienced in attempting to form relationships with people in the host culture. However, retreat into an "ethnic enclave" serves only to temporarily avoid learning about ways to adjust and adapt to the local culture. Although there is no specific time frame that defines this stage of adjustment, there is a pivotal point. International students move from a position of cultural and personal crisis to one of cultural learning and appreciation. This reorientation does not mean that all problems with culture shock end, rather, international students develop the attitude and skills needed for effective problem solving. Access to social support through informal interactions with members of the host culture, or formal social support found in campus programs is a key resource for coping during this phase. Given the nature of issues associated with culture shock, counselors have a key role as "cultural therapists" (Dei, 1992) in assisting international students to resolve challenges associated with cross-cultural transition.

2.2.2.4 Adaptation or Resolution Phase

The adjustment process in cross-cultural transition can be a slow and evolving process. The fourth phase of culture shock depicts *adaptation* or *resolution* of many transition demands (Pedersen, 1995a; Winkelman, 1994). Variation in the adaptation to cross-cultural transition can be explained by four different styles, based upon the extent to which international students maintain their original cultural identity and the extent to which they engage in participation with other cultural groups (Berry, 1985, 1997). Some international students do not either want to or who are unable to hold on to their original cultural identity and typically *assimilate* to the new culture. In contrast, international students who strive to maintain their original cultural identity and who do not actively engage in new cultural contexts adopt a position of *separation*. Alternatively, if avenues for maintaining traditional cultural identity are blocked and there are barriers that prevent international students from joining groups in the new culture, a sense of *exclusion or marginalization* is experienced. A fourth acculturation strategy of *integration* refers to an interest in maintaining some degree of one's original culture while participating as an active member of the new culture.

The adaptation stage of cross-cultural transition is characterized by a greater sense of stability as international students experience success in navigating through the new culture and resolving problems. It should not be assumed that positive adaptation requires international students to assimilate to the host culture. However, it may be the expectation of members of the host culture that international students assimilate to local systems and norms for behavior. The disorientation of culture shock and power differences between international students and other members of the campus community can create pressure to assimilate to the local environment. International students are often better informed about the values and norms of the local culture. Out of a need to survive and thrive during cross-cultural transition, international students have more at stake in learning about local practices. In contrast, members of the host culture and campus community may be less motivated to learn about the culture of international students. Without a mutual interest, interactions in the host culture are typically unidirectional, promoting assimilation as the expectation (Berry, 1997). At best, this bias presents provides motivation for international students to be immersed in the host culture with the possibility of developing a bicultural identity (Martin & Harrell, 1996). In contrast, many international students miss sharing aspects of their culture with others and this can be detrimental for psychological adjustment. It is unfortunate that many members of the host culture do not view the opportunity to interact with international students as posing the same opportunities for cultural learning and personal growth.

2.2.3   Cultural Learning

There are many individual ways that international students resolve their experience of cultural differences. A common factor is the impact of cultural learning (Berry, 1997, Ho, 1995) on personal identity development. Through exposure to a new culture, international students can experience profound personal changes that inevitably lead to incorporating aspects of the new culture into one's personal identity. The development of a bi-cultural identity through integration into the host culture (Berry, 1997) is a significant achievement that represents the ongoing process of managing cultural transition. International students have the potential capacity for effectively managing contrasting and often competing ways of living. Developing cultural flexibility is both a means and end for adapting to culture shock. For many international students, adaptation to the new culture poses more challenges than they ever imagined, however, the personal learning that occurs may also exceed their expectations.

The experience of transition provides individuals with opportunities for learning new ways of relating and responding in cross-cultural contexts (Berry, 1997; Furnham & Bochner, 1986). It is through experiencing cultural differences that international students transform views about themselves and the world around them. Although the experience of culture shock ranges from exhilaration to severe discomfort, living in a new culture provides opportunities for immense cultural learning (Draguns, 1996; Furnham & Bochner, 1986; Pedersen, 1995a).

2.3   Culture Shock as a Syndrome of Stress

Culture shock can be characterized as both a process within cross-cultural transition and as a syndrome of stress. It is important for counselors to be familiar with the ways in which culture shock may manifest in stress-related symptoms. International students are immediately immersed into a new culture that requires learning and adjustment to new role demands. The need for rapid understanding and demonstration of appropriate role behavior in the host culture may be the source of considerable stress, resulting in identity diffusion and role conflict, both of which has been associated with severe culture shock (Pedersen, 1991). Culture shock occurs in response to the numerous stressors that international students perceive during contact with a different culture, when their repertoire of copings strategies are inadequate (Lazarus, 1997). Initial conceptualizations of culture shock (Oberg, 1960) emphasized the strain and feelings of anxiety and confusion that can result from contact with the host culture and the loss of usual cultural cues and social rules. Therefore, the "personal shock" that transpires from crossing cultures is a process that derives from both the challenge of managing in the new culture and the loss of familiar cultural surroundings (Winkelman, 1994).

Six defining characteristics associated with culture shock are relevant for understanding the experiences of international students (Pedersen, 1988, 1990).

- Familiar cues about how an international student is supposed to behave may not be available or they have new meaning in the host culture;
- Disruption to the individual's value system occurs through exposure to conflicting ideas about important values and desired behavior;
- Culture shock inevitably results in a state of emotional tension that can range from mild irritability and fatigue to stronger and sometimes alarming reactions such as uncontrollable rage or anxiety;
- Culture shock may heighten the individual's comparison between home and host cultures and a longing for the way things "used to be";
- Coping skills that are usually effective for personal management may not be effective for coping in new cultural contexts. This can derail a sense of personal competency and lead international students to question their decision to take on the challenge of cross-cultural transition; and,

- Culture shock is a process within cross-cultural transition. Although international students may desire immediate relief from distressing symptoms, they cannot remove themselves from the host culture without giving up their student status. It may provide hope for international students to realize that culture shock is likely to dissipate once they have mastered competencies for understanding and responding to cues in the host environment. This is a process that occurs over time and international students need both time and resources to master new ways of responding to the demands of cross-cultural transition.

2.3.1   Normalizing Culture Shock

An important point worth reiterating is that culture shock is a normal response to change during cross-cultural transition (Pedersen, 1995a). Difficulties are enhanced when international students are not prepared for the personal impact of moving to new cultural surroundings. People who are highly competent in their life roles, e.g., student, worker, may presume that their abilities will automatically generalize to effectively managing in a new cultural context. However, the cognitive and psychological reactions to new culture extend beyond the usual skills practiced in life roles. Rather, it is the capacity of international students to adjust their usual ways of perceiving and responding in the new environment that is essential for cross-cultural competence (Arthur, 1997). International students can be assisted through psychoeducational approaches that provide information about the syndrome of culture shock, emphasizing that it is a normal response to cross-cultural transition. International students experience tremendous relief when counselors normalize their experiences and when they gain perspective about their experience of culture shock. However, international students require more than assurance that their experiences are "normal". They require interventions to assist with symptom relief and to increase their repertoire of coping strategies for managing perceived demands in the local environment (Chen, 1999).

2.3.2   Symptoms of Culture Shock

International students entering a new cultural context may suffer from cognitive overload and the associated fatigue (Guthrie, 1975; Winkelman, 1994). In familiar cultural environments, cognitive and sensory processes normally operate through automatic and unconscious processing of information. However, in unfamiliar cultural environments, a conscious and deliberate effort must be made to process and understand the meaning of new information. International students can expend considerable mental and physical energy on hypervigilant monitoring of new surroundings. Until they are able to sort out the relative importance of cues in the local environment, including social interactions, the energy expended in daily interactions can lead to fatigue. Coupled with the effort that it takes for students to manage their interactions using a second language, it not surprising that a classic symptom of culture shock is exhaustion. International students may lack the terminology for naming the syndrome of culture shock but nonetheless present a myriad of stress-related psychological and physiological symptoms (see Table 1).

Table 1. Common Psychological And Physiological Symptoms Of Culture Shock

Anger	Insecure
Anxiety	Insomnia
Cognitive impairment	Irritability
Confusion	Lack of energy
Curiosity Exhaustion	Loneliness
Defensiveness	Loss of appetite
Depression	Loss of control
Disorientation	Mood Swings
Excitement	Muscle tension
Exhaustion	Overeating
Fatigue	Resentment
Fear	Sadness
Gastrointestinal problems	Sense of loss
Headaches	Unfamiliar body pain
Homesickness	Vague bodily sensations
Inferiority	Withdrawal

Culture shock manifests in psychological symptoms such as depression, social withdrawal, academic problems, loneliness, hostility towards host culture members, or physiological reactions such as sleep disturbances, gastrointestinal problems, or other vague physical symptoms (Thomas & Althen, 1989; Winkelman, 1994). The expression of stress-related symptoms is learned through notions about cultural acceptability. Some international students find it more acceptable to divulge physiological, rather than psychological symptoms (Furnham & Bochner, 1986; Mallinckrodt & Leong, 1992, Zhang, 1995). "Presenting with a body part as the cause of distress is culturally determined; it also allows the student to avoid feelings of shame or social isolation" (Aubrey, 1991, p. 29). Counselors need to be aware of the symptoms commonly associated with the experience of culture shock, particularly tendencies to somatically experience symptoms of culture shock. Although culture shock increases the likelihood of both psychosomatic and physical illness, symptoms should be taken seriously. A close working relationship with campus medical services is essential to assist students to access appropriate treatment for their health concerns.

2.3.3   Culture Shock Can Be Positive

Although the discussion has focused on some of the more debilitating aspects of culture shock, a clarification is in order. The goal of interventions with people in cross-cultural transition is not to eradicate the experience of culture shock; that may not be even possible or desirable. The same contrasts between the home and host cultures that contribute to culture shock also lead to profound learning. It is the opportunity for learning that lead many students to seek out educational programs in foreign countries. Cross-cultural transition may be more difficult than students ever imagined or planned. However, success at overcoming cultural barriers and learning new ways of interacting can be extremely rewarding. Culture shock is therefore a double-sided feature of cross-cultural transition; it is the most stressful and the most motivating aspect of living and learning in a new cultural environment.

2.4   Chapter Summary

International students can be characterized as learners in transition. Depending upon the discrepancy between norms and sources of social support available to students in the home and host countries, the transition to a novel cultural environment is usually accompanied by a reaction characterized by culture shock. Their temporary status as sojourners in a foreign country is the basis for complex issues that emerge during the initial period of adjustment through to the re-entry transition of returning home. The demands for acculturation to the local environment frequently overtax international students' available coping resources. Although the demands of cross-cultural transitions may require international students to make difficult adjustments, there is potential for profound learning and personal growth. Counselors who are familiar with models of transition can have a stronger appreciation for the context surrounding adjustment issues. The demands of living and learning in a foreign country include both common adjustment issues and unique issues based on the individual circumstances of international students. In the next chapter, common issues experienced by international students during cross-cultural transition to the host culture are reviewed.

3

The Transition Issues of International Students

3. INTERNATIONAL STUDENTS AS LEARNERS IN TRANSITION

International students are people in transition. International students must manage the transition away from their home country, manage the transition to living and learning in a new country, manage the transition of leaving the host country, and then manage the transition home. Their status as temporary sojourners in a foreign country for the duration of an academic program is a unique condition of their cross-cultural experience. Students "begin" the transition process through applying to foreign institutions, acquiring immigration authorization, gathering financial and other resources, making travel arrangements, and preparing to leave family and friends. Therefore, prior to departure for the host country, international students have invested considerable effort into their cross-cultural experience. Family members or sponsorship agencies such as government and employers are often personally or financially invested in an individual's decision to become an international student.

3.1 Reasons for Becoming an International Student

The circumstances surrounding a decision to study in foreign countries are helpful for understanding students' experiences of transition in the host culture. For example, conditions in the home country have been linked to students' academic preparation and their motivation for academic success (Thomas & Althen, 1989). Although some international students may be selected to study abroad due to their superior academic qualifications, others desire the experience of living in another country, or their family has influence in local government or sponsoring agencies. Local political conditions may also be the impetus for making the transition to another country. It is not uncommon for families to send one or more children abroad due to conditions of war or oppressive practices of local governments. In light of the variety of circumstances that prompt the decision to study abroad, commonly held perceptions about international students must be challenged. As noted in Chapter 1, assumptions about international students representing the "cream of the crop" in terms of academic goals and abilities may hold true for some students, whereas other students will be less motivated and unprepared for the rigors of studying in a foreign environment. The lives of international students from countries around the world are varied. Conditions in industrialized nations and those deemed "third world" impact both the desirability of foreign education and the financial resources to sponsor students (Dei, 1992). Both political and economic factors in the home country can be influential for decisions to become an international student and impact the experience of living in a foreign country.

3.2   Academic Preparation

Points raised in this discussion challenge the tendency to treat individual students as a homogeneous group of learners. It is important to explore within group differences and keep sight of the tremendous variability in the academic and personal preparation of international students. Although there are common influences on cross-cultural transition, individual circumstances impact the experience of living and learning in a foreign country. On the other hand, there has also been a tendency to emphasize the differences between international students and learners from the host culture. In reality, international students have many of the same issues to manage as local students who are adjusting to role demands in the transition to new educational programs (Arthur & Hiebert, 1996; Barker, Child, Gallois, Jones, & Callan, 1991; Hayes & Lin, 1994). However, the educational transition for international students is compounded by the simultaneous demands of cultural transition (Alexander & Shaw, 2001; Leong & Chou, 1996). At the same time as international students are managing new educational programs, they are also adjusting to cultural differences between educational methodologies in their home and the host country. Added to this are many demands to master changes in other roles of daily living in the host culture. The complexity of cultural transitions mean that international students are likely to experience more problems than students from the host culture. As a general rule, the greater the difference between home and host cultures, the greater the adjustment demands faced by international students (Pedersen, 1991). Access to usual ways of coping may be restricted and students may be unfamiliar with coping resources in the local campus and community environments. However, given the sheer number of countries and cultures involved in international education, it should not be assumed that students experience cross-cultural transitions as equally stressful (Wan et al., 1992; Tanaka, Takai, Kohyama, & Fuhihara, 1994). Counselors need to consider both the common and unique experiences of international students in cross-cultural transition.

The goal of this chapter is to discuss several key transition issues that are commonly faced by international students in their adjustment to living and learning in a foreign country. The transition issues elaborated upon in this chapter include academic concerns, communication issues, social support, family matters, discrimination, gender roles, and financial support. Followed by the discussion of these common transition themes, the interrelationship between academic success and cross-cultural success will be outlined. The intent of reviewing common transition issues is not to ignore the unique aspects of international students' perspectives. General knowledge can provide counselors with a foundation from which to explore the specific nature of international student experiences during cross-cultural transition.

3.3   Common Transition Issues

3.3.1   Academic Goals as a Central Concern

As noted in the introduction to this chapter, there are major investments made in the decision to become an international student. Many international students leave their family, friends, and familiar roles and sources of support behind in order to study in another country. Success is dependent upon the capacity of international students to manage their academic program of study. Consequently, the stress experienced by many international learners pivots around academic concerns (Wan et al., 1992). What is at stake for the international student is more than pressure for academic success. The threat of failure, whether real of perceived, and returning home to face embarrassment of self, family, or sponsors, coupled with responsibilities for financial resources are immense pressures (Wehrly, 1988). Counselors must consider that academic concerns have far-reaching implications for an international student. Due to the contingency of immigration status based upon academic success, the threat of failure can be overwhelming pressure (Arthur, 1997). Early intervention with international students is highly desirable to prevent the potentially devastating consequences of having to return home before completing an academic program.

Academic concerns represent the major transition issue faced by international students (Walker, 1999). The academic concerns commonly expressed by international students include prior academic preparation, adjustment to foreign teaching methodology, pressure from performance expectations, curriculum content, and workload issues (Barker et al., 1991; Jochems, Snippe, Smid, & Verseij, 1996; Liberman, 1994; Petress, 1995; Walker, 1999. With respect to prior academic preparation, considerable variation exists in the educational background of students who are admitted to foreign educational programs. Some students rank in the top levels of school programs in their home countries and these students are used to being top achievers. The challenges of a new curriculum may disrupt prior levels of academic success and create added pressures for redefining personal competencies. International students may miss the status that they previous held as an outstanding performer in their home community.

3.3.1.1 Competition for International Students

Several challenges have been made against the assumption that international students represent the "best and the brightest" of their country (Thomas & Althen, 1989). First, many of the best students choose to remain in their own countries and pursue the limited spaces available in post-secondary programs. Second, many countries around the world have made educational reform a priority. Where resources have supported large-scale scholarship programs, i.e., in oil-rich nations, increasing opportunities have been made available for greater numbers of students, including those with modest academic preparation. A third factor related to changes in the international student population is related to the recent emphasis on higher education as a global commodity. With an increasing number of institutions mandating international education programs, the top students have more choice about which country and which educational institution they attend. These points challenge the assumption that international students are a homogeneous group in terms of their levels of academic preparation (Thomas & Althen). As more institutions enter the arena of competition to attract foreign tuition fees, there is increased access into foreign academic programs for greater numbers of international students. This has led to shift in thinking in terms of recruitment and admission practices. Rather than limiting access to students whose background is exceptional, many institutions have established policies around "minimum standards" to increase their numbers of international students. Along with policies directed at admission practices, educational institutions must be prepared to support international students who have a wider range of background preparation and motivation to succeed.

3.1.1.2 Background Preparation

The lack of international standards for educational programs in many countries leads to variability in the knowledge base of students. Expectations about academic performance in a foreign educational system may be unrealistic. For example, the reason that students from many developing countries choose to pursue foreign education is due to limitations in the scope of local curricula (Dei, 1992). However, it should not be assumed that all international students enter foreign institutions in a "deficit" position. It may be the case that prior experience exceeds the curricula in academic programs in the host country. International students whose academic and employment background is more extensive than those of local students may be frustrated about the lack of challenge. In either case, the issue becomes how well the background experience of students matches the curriculum of the foreign academic program. In cases where the gap results in lack of preparation, international students are likely to feel overwhelmed by academic demands. Alternatively, those students who feel they are duplicating prior learning are likely to be frustrated about "wasting their time" and money. These examples illustrate how expectations about academic performance, when either too high or too low, can be critical sources of stress for international students.

3.3.1.3. Teaching and Learning Styles

Expectations for academic performance may not be in line with former achievement levels or foreign teaching methodologies. The classroom environment can be difficult for international students when expectations for learning are not clearly defined and when teaching styles conflict with previous learning experiences. For example, students from countries where teaching methodology is more autocratic in style may miss the usual structure, clear expectations, and the formal lines of authority that are followed during student-teacher transactions (Barker et al., 1991; Sheehan & Pearson, 1995). However, a more "open" teaching method can result in exciting discoveries through the learning through increased interactions between teachers and students (Liberman, 1994). International students from collectivist cultures may also struggle with cultural norms for individual achievement. The same behavior by local students that is rewarded in the classrooms of highly individualistic cultures may seem aggressive to international students and be interpreted as showing an offensive lack of respect.

International students used to a highly organized, lecture style of instruction and a highly structured curriculum may find popular constructivist and collaborative approaches to education to be confusing.

Differences in teaching style and class interactions can tax international students to define their role in a learning process that had previously been defined for them. Some researchers have focused on practical teaching suggestions for addressing communication and cultural differences with international students (Collingridge, 1999; Lee, 1997).

3.3.1.4 Curriculum Relevance

Another influence on the academic experiences of international students are the examples used in classroom discussion to ground theoretical concepts. When examples are derived solely from the host environment or culture, international students may not be able to relate to the example or they may feel that they are being excluded from the discussion (Huxur, Mansfield, Nnazor, Schuetze, & Segawa, 1996). One unfortunate outcome of culturally exclusive curriculum is that it leads international students to conclude that the curriculum is irrelevant to their life circumstances. Another unfortunate outcome is that international students feel like they do not belong in the local academic context.

3.3.1.5 Academic Counseling is Multifaceted

Counselors are cautioned against assuming that all international students will have the same adjustment issues in managing academic demands. Rather, this is dependent upon what individual students perceive to be stressful and also how they appraise their coping resources to deal with those demands (Arthur & Hiebert, 1993). For example, students who rate their language skills as adequate are more likely to report academic situations as less stressful than students who perceive their language skills to be weaker. Confidence in academic ability and confidence in problem-solving skills can also mitigate international students' appraisals of academic stress (Wan et al., 1992).

Counselors need to attend to international students' academic goals and expectations for success, particularly at the beginning of the academic year when students are immersed in their foreign education (Volet & Renshaw, 1995). This is a particularly vulnerable time for international students as they may be coping with information overload and lack of familiarity with procedures and resources within the educational institution (Westwood & Barker, 1990). International students may have exceedingly high expectations for academic success that are driven by their personal standards for success or by what they believe others expect of them. In other studies of student populations (Arthur & Hayward, 1997; Flett, Blankstein, Hewitt, & Koledin, 1992), learners who hold unrealistically high expectations regarding academic achievement struggle to sustain academic success and are prone to debilitating anxiety and depression. To date, the influence of perfectionist beliefs has not been studied in international student populations. However, the circumstances that lead to international study, the high levels of personal investment, and the accompanying expectations of others appear as background conditions that could easily lead to unrealistic standards for academic performance. Expectations for performance may not be in line with the students' academic or personal preparation for managing in a foreign culture (Huxur et al., 1996).

3.3.2   Communication Problems

The majority of international students choose to study in a foreign language. Language proficiency has been consistently linked to both the academic and social adjustment of international students (e.g., Hayes & Lin, 1994; Jochems, Snippe, Smid, & Verweij, 1996; Tanaka, Takai, Kohyama, Fujihara & Minami, 1997; Ying & Liese, 1990). Students with stronger language skills have better capacity for managing academic demands and are less likely to view those demands as stressful (Wan et al., 1992). There are several issues pertaining to communication during cross-cultural transitions. These are categorized as the skills, motivations, and interpretations that influence intercultural communication competence (Zimmermann, 1995).

3.3.2.1 Communication Competency

Communication issues during cross-cultural transitions are complex and involve competencies on many levels. From a review of intercultural communication literature, six overriding components of competency have been identified: Social decentering, knowledge of the host culture, language competence, adaptation, communication effectiveness, and social integration (Redmond, 2000; Redmond & Bunyi, 1993). Social decentering refers to understanding and adapting to those who are culturally different. International students who communicate from a monocultural perspective are limited in their abilities to communicate in ways that make sense to members of other cultures. Related to the capacity for social decentering is knowledge about the host culture. Knowing something about the other culture's history, values, and non-verbal norms is extremely important for reducing the level of anxiety around social appropriateness and for minimizing intercultural misunderstandings. Language competency is considered as of the most influential factors in the cross-cultural experience of international students. However, it appears that confidence in using one's language ability is at least as important as measures of actual ability in determining student adjustment (Ying & Liese, 1990). Intercultural communication has also been linked to successful adaptation (Redmond & Bunyi, 1993). The extent to which international students are able to adapt to different points of view and be interpersonally flexible when confronted by cultural differences is strongly tied to language capacity. A reciprocal relationship exists between communication effectiveness and intercultural competence. International students' competency for communicating in the host culture impacts both their sense of confidence about approaching host nationals and the quality of social interactions (Huxur et al., 1996). The capacity for intercultural communication has a major influence on social integration and the degree to which international students are able to engage in the social networks of the host culture (Redmond & Bunyi, 1993).

Effective communication in host country is essential for international students to benefit from their chosen program of study. However, programs designed to assist international students need to consider that intercultural communication is multidimensional in nature. The effectiveness of academic and support programs designed to assist international students may be limited if students do not possess the requisite language skills or the confidence to use those skills (Wan et al., 1992). Through assessing the cognitive, affective and behavioral dimensions of intercultural communication competence, interventions can be tailored to meet the specific needs of international students (Zimmermann, 1995).

3.3.2.2 Language Skills for Academic Success

Intercultural communication competence is more complex than a single focus on language proficiency. Nonetheless, the emphasis on language proficiency has led most educational institutions to establish policies that require international students to provide evidence of meeting standards as a condition of admission, i.e., language test scores. However, there are considerable variations in the admission policies of institutions of higher learning and the extent to which standards regarding language proficiency are rigidly adhered to (Cownie & Addison, 1996). Recently, some educational institutions have attempted to increase international student access through offering a two-tiered policy on language proficiency. Students who meet the minimum standard can be admitted to full-time studies in the chosen academic program. Students whose language skills are below the minimum standard for full-time studies may be offered probationary admission status with a modified academic program. In the latter case, international students may be offered a "half and half" curriculum in which they are part-time students in an academic stream while devoting the rest of their time at the educational institution upgrading their language skills. Weak language skills inevitably increase the level of difficulty in entering a foreign culture. However, the advantage here is that students may be able to have a head start in their academic program while upgrading their language skills and adjusting to the local culture (Cownie & Addison, 1996).

Communication issues have also been discussed in relation to specific academic behaviors of international students. The stereotypical view of international students is that they are reticent to initiate classroom discussion and limit their participation to brief exchanges (Tapper, 1996). However, what might appear on the surface to be problems of language proficiency might actually be an issue of cultural proficiency on behalf of the international students, instructors, and other students. When classroom or seminar discussion is closely connected to local cultural contexts, international students may find it difficult to know how to contribute to discussion (Huxur et al., 1996). If they believe that their basis of knowledge or experience is culturally irrelevant for the discussion, international students will be reticent about attempting to contribute. Instructors and other students may unintentionally exclude international students by limiting their discussion to narrow examples found in local cultural contexts. A lack of awareness or training by faculty to apply theoretical knowledge to broader cultural contexts may be prohibitive for international students and restrict the learning that can occur for all students.

At the same time that international students are dealing with a difficult cultural environment, they may have difficulties articulating their concerns of adjustment. Limited knowledge of the language used in the host culture may restrict their expression of private thoughts and feelings (Clark Oropeza, Fitzgibbon, & Baron, 1991). Communication barriers may pose additional challenges for international students in terms of their interaction with members of the host culture and for accessing social support. The discussion in Chapter 7 elaborates upon the impact of language proficiency in counseling.

3.3.3   Building Social Support

Cross-cultural transitions often result in a lack of personal validation, cultural conflicts, and loss of cultural attachment (Ishiyama, 1995a). In making the transition to another country, international students not only lose their traditional sources of self- validation; they may also be deprived of the familiar means through which social support is communicated. The loss of emotional and social support systems that occurs through the transition to another country can result in intense feelings of homesickness (McKinlay, Pattison, & Gross, 1996; Pedersen, 1991; Sandhu & Asrabadi, 1994). If sources of support are inadequate during the process of cross-cultural transition, international students may experience debilitating stress (Mallinckrodt & Leong, 1992; Wan et al., 1992).

Social support is a powerful coping resource for people who are managing life transitions (Schlossberg, 1984) and is particularly important managing the stress associated with cross-cultural transitions (Martin & Harrell, 1996; Ward & Kennedy, 1993). Research suggests that social support has both direct effects on psychological adjustment and buffering effects for mitigating the impact of life stresses (Lazarus & Folkman, 1984). For international students, lack of social support is a direct source of stress and, conversely, the availability of social support has a positive impact. When international students feel overtaxed by the demands perceived in the new culture, social support can help to buffer or moderate the impact of those demands. In either case, if sources of support are inadequate, international students may experience high levels of stress. Given the associations established between social support and psychological adjustment (Lazarus & Folkman, 1984, it is important to consider how international students may be helped or hindered through social support.

3.3.3.1. Accessing Social Support

International students often experience feelings ranging from reluctance to anxiety about their need to access social support in the host culture. The reasons for their hesitancy can be related to concerns about language competency and about what constitutes socially appropriate behavior in new cultural contexts. Mismatches between international students and host members expectations and perceptions of behavior can lead to strong affect related to social alienation (Wong-Rieger, 1984).

International students are likely to seek assistance from the people whom they have the most contact with and whom they believe is approachable. It has been reported that faculty members are the main people that international students approach for problem solving academic and personal issues (Mallinckrodt & Leong, 1992). Similar to the coping patterns identified with local students (Arthur & Hiebert, 1996), male international students tend to have more positive relationships with faculty members than females, and females tend to focus their social support needs on family members and specific academic needs (Mallinckrodt & Leong, 1992). Gender differences in patterns of seeking social support may be instructive for designing counseling services for international students.

3.3.3.2 Friendships with Co-Nationals

International students have been criticized for forming groups with others from similar cultural backgrounds or from nations with geographical proximity. It may appear to others that students are rejecting opportunities for cross-cultural learning and affiliation. However, the experience of many international students is that developing friendships with local students is a difficult and disappointing experience (Walker, 1999). International students from collectivist cultures may be confused by the patterns of interaction found in cultures that are more individualistic in nature (Barker et al., 1991; Cross, 1995). For example, individualist cultures sanction many levels of friendship with varying degrees of responsibilities, attachments, and relationship intensity. In contrast, students from collectivist cultures are used to having greater intensity of friendships with fewer people, but value the stability of those relationships (Triandis, 1989). International students who prefer higher levels of interdependence may be frustrated by the apparent superficiality of interactions in a host culture that appears to be dominated by a concern with time and activity (Arthur, 1997). As one international student expressed, "People here ask how you are, but then keep on walking by!" Where there is more similarity between international students' home culture and practices in the local culture, there is less hesitancy about pursuing social interaction.

In light of some of the difficulties with cross-cultural friendships, it should not be assumed that foreign students naturally gravitate towards people of the same nationality. Differences in temperament, personality and interests will impact the degree of compatibility between students. The ethnocentric tendency to lump international students together and assume that they have mutual interests should be avoided (Clark Oropeza et al., 1991). Differences such as political, religious, and social conflicts that originate from home countries can play out through alliances and conflicts in the host country (Thomas & Althen, 1989). There is no reason to believe that students from countries that have historically been divided will engage in cordial relationships in another setting. For example, during a social event organized for international students, the author witnessed the transfer of political strife into the local setting. Two students from Vietnam were introduced to each other. Immediately, one of the students asked the other, "What part of Vietnam are you from?" The historical division of Vietnam was enacted as one of the students emphatically commented, "We are from different parts of Vietnam", and deliberately avoided further contact with the other student. This example serves to highlight the need for campus personnel to have an understanding of the relationships between countries of origin and the internal politics that can potentially impact international students' social relations. Knowledge of both intergroup and intragroup alliances is useful for appreciating the social relationships of international students.

3.3.3.3 Support for International Friendships

It should not be assumed that merely bringing international and local students together on the same campus automatically results in cross-cultural friendships. Solely relying on proximity and time together on the same campus to promote intercultural exchanges is most often insufficient. Language barriers and value differences require additional time, commitment, and personal confidence by both parties to overcome those differences and to find common understandings and mutual interests (Furnham & Alibhai, 1985). Positive social interactions can influence international students' view of the host culture. Beyond general influences, positive interactions can also assist students' social adjustment and satisfaction with their educational experience (Kamal & Maruyama, 1990). However, rather than viewing social involvement as solely the responsibility of the international student, students in the host culture need to be motivated to develop competencies for building cross-cultural friendships. Students in the host culture may have a monocultural view of the world and lack both sensitivity and experience with diverse racial and ethnic groups to bridge international friendships (Hayes & Lin, 1994). Programs designed to facilitate international friendships are helpful to prepare students for sustaining cross-cultural relationships (Saidla & Grant, 1993).

Whereas international students may desire more contact with students, their experiences, particularly early in the host culture, may lack the intimate qualities of friendships that lead to a sense of belonging. Making friends with local students is one of the most difficult and least successful areas of adjustment (Walker, 1999). Coupled with the demands of academic systems and studying in a second language, it is little wonder that international students seek reprieve in the familiarity of others who share language and other cultural similarities (Bochner, Hutnik, & Furnham, 1985; Furnham & Alibhai, 1985). Relationships with co-nationals may be an essential source of support for international students. It makes sense that international students will approach those they feel most comfortable with for resolving problems of adjustment. It may be easier for international students to confide to a co-national than less familiar people on campus. However, there may be times when international students wish to keep their personal problems confidential from co-national peers and be more likely to seek assistance from "outsiders", including counseling services (Pedersen, 1991). What becomes apparent is that supportive relationships do not necessarily develop merely as a function of people coming together on campus. Rather, both international and local students may benefit from campus programming designed to promote positive interactions in cross-cultural exchanges (Nesdale & Todd, 2000).

3.3.4   Costs of Living in a Foreign Country

Financial restraint in higher education has eliminated many of the subsidies that were formerly available to international students through bursary or scholarship program. Recruitment efforts have been redirected towards those students who can finance the full costs of their foreign education. Differential tuition fees and changes in the costs of daily living require a major financial commitment by international students. Students studying in another country with a comparable standard of living to their home country will have fewer financial adjustments. However, where there is a shift in the costs of living between their home and host countries, there are associated financial issues (Walker, 1999). In some cases, students cross cultures and have a financial advantage in the host setting. However, students who have enjoyed a relatively high standard of living in their home countries but face higher costs of living in the host culture are more likely to experience issues of adjustment. Coming to the host country can threaten both the financial and social status that these students have grown accustomed to at home (Akande, 1994; Clark Oropeza et al., 1991). Changes in standards of living can be an overriding factor for international students' experience of the host culture. A means of financial support and financial stability are critical factors for the economic viability of living in a new cultural setting and a sense of personal satisfaction (Berry, 1997).

3.3.4.1 Availability of Financial Resources

Although many international students finance their overseas education through the resources of their family, it should not be assumed that students come from wealthy families. Many international students receive financial support from their local government, extended family, or a foreign sponsor. Families may endure considerable financial hardship to send one of their children abroad (Pedersen, 1991). In such cases, resources are extremely limited and students experience additional pressures with respect to their sense of family obligations for success. International students who struggle to meet the high costs of living in the host country for basic items such as food and clothing may be reluctant to request assistance that would place a further burden on family resources. Financial stressors distract international students from their academic studies and adversely impact their sense of stability (Walker, 1999). Programming regarding the cost differentials between home and local communities, responsible consumerism, budgeting skills, and resources for low-cost purchases are important topics for student orientation.

3.3.5   Discrimination and Racism

During cross-cultural transition, international students may be exposed to the negative influences of discrimination and racism (Dei, 1992; Sandu & Asrabadi, 1994). Prejudice between groups of international students or alienation from the dominant group of the host culture are major influences on the acculturation of international students (Sodowsky & Plake, 1992). Upon arriving to a host country, some international students face abrupt changes in their social status due to the racial composition of the local population. For some students, the shift from being members of the "majority race" to minority status represents the first time in their lives that they have personally confronted racism. International students who are members of racial and ethnic minorities are exposed to the attitudes and stereotypes held by members of the local community. Negative stereotypes regarding particular countries and people around the world may be transferred to international students through subtle forms of bias or through blatant hostility.

3.3.5.1 Institutional Forms of Discrimination

Institutional racism and discrimination are also evident in the policies, practices, and curriculum of educational institutions. For example, policies pertaining to employment for international students may appear on the surface as creating opportunities for gaining foreign work experience. In reality, however, hiring practices are extremely restrictive. The terms of student visas in most countries prohibit employment outside of academic program requirements, i.e., practicum, field work (Walker, 1999). Some campuses have developed employment policies that permit the hiring of international students in campus positions offered to the entire student population, for example as teaching assistants. However, qualifications for employment typically advantage students with local work experience; international students face unequal terms for job competitiveness. In cases of personal hardship, counselors can assist through networking with campus personnel to encourage favorable hiring practices with international students. However, it is important that work experience builds upon occupational skills and does not result in underemployment in menial tasks.

Beyond the borders of campus, entry into local employment opportunities may be prohibitive due to immigration rules in the country (Dei, 1992). For example, international students in Canada face a "catch 22" dilemma in securing employment. On the one hand, employers are legally prohibited from hiring international students unless they have received proper immigration authorization. On the other hand, immigration officials will not issue a work permit until student presents confirmation of employment. There is uncertainty about whether students will receive authorization and when they will actually be available for work. From the employer's point of view, holding a job for an international student does not make sense when domestic employees are readily available. Immigration policies in Canada are currently under review to revise some of the restrictions placed on the employment of international students.

3.3.5.2 Cultural Encapsulation in Curriculum

The content of curriculum and materials in educational programs are potential sources of discrimination against international students. First, curriculum may be based upon ethnocentric views of academic subjects that attest to one "right way" of understanding the world. In the main countries that receive international students, there are biases towards Eurocentrism, at the expense of contributions made by non-European societies (Dei, 1992). This lack of representation silences learning about diverse practices in other parts of the world. Second, curriculum is often outdated about the norms and practices of people from other countries, or highlights problems reported in the media. Imagine what it must be like for students from developing countries to attend classes in which their communities and countries are generalized as 'backward' or 'plagued with problems'. International students who feel embarrassed about the portrayal of their country may be reluctant to challenge the accuracy of information, especially if that means confronting instructors or other persons perceived to be in positions of power.

The discrimination faced by international students is frequently due to limited and biased information that campus personnel have about source countries. Training materials used to sensitize staff to the background of international students, i.e., cultural briefs, provide introductory material but typically only a superficial view of life in that country. For example, one international student advisor relayed the reactions of international students to cultural information that was prepared for instructors. Although this particular group of students chose to find humor in the portrayal of their country, student services staff had to manage their personal embarrassment for contributing to stereotypical information. At best, general information about the source countries of international students countries provides an overview of cultural practices. However, if campus personnel do not take the time to learn more about the backgrounds of international students, their good intentions may be overshadowed by unintentional racism (Pedersen, 1995b).

3.3.5.3 Status and Power Differences

International students may face discrimination and racism as specific actions directed towards students from specific regions of the world, or directed towards them as a group. The experiences of international students are perhaps best understood as the degree to which they share power and status with other groups on campus. International students are situated at the lower end of a hierarchy of power and priority on many campuses (Dei, 1992). One contributing factor to the power imbalance is the view that international learners represent an 'extra' or 'other' group of students on campus. The positioning of international students apart from the mainstream student population immediately introduces differences in status and power, thereby allocating international students to the position of minority group. Campus internationalization programs are faced with the challenge of educating campus personnel about the importance role that international learners have in post-secondary education. Until the attitudes of campus personnel and the campus infrastructure to support this student group change, their position of power on campus is likely to remain tenuous. International students need to be viewed as integral members of the campus community. As long as international students are relegated to a subordinate position, their experience will most likely include both subtle and overt oppression expressed through discrimination and racism. Regardless of the type of oppression, it poses a barrier for international students in the attainment of their educational and personal goals.

3.3.6   Gender Role Expectations

There are cultural differences regarding expectations for male-female relationships. Moving to a country with more "liberated" views of social norms for interacting can be disconcerting (Clark Oropeza et al., 1991). Especially for students from male-dominated cultures, or where public expression of affection is frowned upon or forbidden, there are sharp contrasts in definitions of acceptable behavior in the host country. Exposure to feminism can exert powerful influences on students' perceptions and attitudes towards gender roles (Matsui, 1988). Gender role expectations for behavior may be questioned through new ways of interacting, experimentation with behavior and testing boundaries about acceptable sexual behavior (Tyler & Boxer, 1996).

3.3.6.1 Women International Students

Research on international populations is fairly consistent in the finding that females hold more liberal attitudes about the rights and roles of women than do males (Gibbons, Stiles, & Shkodriani, 1991). Females may see the potential advantages of equality for women, particularly in terms of freedom and personal rights. In contrast, males may prefer the status quo and the power traditionally assigned to male privilege. The limited numbers of studies addressing gender differences in the experiences of international students generally show that female students experience higher levels of distress (Mallinckrodt & Leong, 1992). Possible explanations may be that female students have greater adjustments in moving between countries in terms of gender role behavior, they may have greater role conflict in the expectations to carry both family and student responsibilities, and there is a lack of campus programming to address role strain. The risks for psychological health may involve "double jeopardy" for female international students.

3.3.6.2 Sexual Behavior

The increasing number of international students studying abroad means that students are bringing diverse notions of gender appropriate behavior to institutions of higher learning. The interpretation of verbal and nonverbal behavior varies between cultures, including the expression of sexual behavior (Tyler & Boxer, 1996). As campuses promote policies and consciousness-raising programs designed for the prevention and remediation of sexual harassment, it is imperative that international students be educated about appropriate and inappropriate behavior in the host culture. Part of the dilemma here is that there are many inconsistencies in "what counts" as either appropriate or inappropriate sexual behavior in many countries. There can be variations in what behavior is adjudicated as sexual harassment and there can be wide variations in what is deemed acceptable behavior by members of the local culture. Shifting role boundaries for men and women in the local culture can be doubly confusing for international students who are attempting to figure out the nuances of social interaction. Nonetheless, cross-cultural miscommunication results in serious consequences for international students if their behavior is adjudicated as sexual harassment. If international students are informed about campus policies and local practices, they may be assisted to avoid cross-cultural misunderstandings concerning sexual behavior (Tyler & Boxer, 1996).

3.3.6.3 Challenging Western Views

The majority of literature available on international student mobility is written from the point for view of students entering more "liberal" countries in North America and Europe. However, increasing opportunities for study abroad programs in other countries throughout the world mean that students may be crossing cultures where distinct gender role behavior is the norm. Students must be prepared by becoming informed about local practices and views of expected behavior for men and women. Without prior knowledge, students may be shocked at the ways in which women and men are differentially treated. Students may need to modify their typical ways of dressing or interacting in public in order to reduce the risk of being culturally offensive. Through developing an understanding of local practices, students can be helped to situate behavior in a cross-cultural context and be less prone to evaluate gender expectations from the point of view of practices in their home culture.

3.3.7 Family Matters

The common adjustment issues of international students are typically centered on the experience of the individual. However, individual adjustment is strongly connected to the well being of significant others. For some individuals, becoming an international student means resolving the choice of leaving family members behind. Imagine a student who has always lived in the family home and who must for the first time navigate life without the immediate support of family members in a new country! Other students may be faced with the dilemma of leaving their spouse and children for an extended period of time. Feelings of loneliness and preoccupation with the well being of family members can be major sources of stress for international students (Parr et al., 1992).

In cases where finances do not permit visiting the home country, there is absence from family for several years. International students have concerns about missing the celebration of family milestones and about being with their families in times of crisis. For example, one of the most difficult situations for international students is the loss of a loved one during their sojourn to another country. Grieving is more difficult if the student cannot return to their home country for the funeral or death rituals. Along with grief, there may be other matters of family ritual, role responsibilities, and community representation that weigh heavily from afar. For others, the birth of children conceived while at home, or other family rites of passage are events that trigger homesickness.

3.3.7.1 Families in Transition

Many international students travel to the host country with family members. However, campus programs frequently neglect family members who accompany international students (Mallinckrodt & Leong, 1992; Siegel, 1991). Issues of status, role change, language proficiency, legal ability to work, and social isolation may be paramount for family members. An issue that has not been widely acknowledged in is the differential rate of acculturation between the family members of international students (Clark Oropeza et al., 1991). Children of families in cross-cultural transition typically acculturate at a faster rate than their parents. Depending upon the degree of exposure by family members to the local culture, their language proficiency, and the effort expended to assimilate to local ways, there can be wide variations in their experiences. Research on families of immigrant children (e.g., Baptise, 1990, 1993) is instructive for understanding the issues related to family transition. Exposure to new cultural norms challenges the typical ways in which families manage roles, traditions, and lines of authority. International students may have different ideas than their family members about incorporating new cultural practices into the family unit.

Acculturation on the family system should not be ignored because there are profound influences on international students' academic and personal success. When family tension results, international students are distracted from a focus on academic achievement. Counselors should be aware of family issues that occur from development issues such as moving away from the family unit and those accelerated through exposure to new or conflicting values in the host culture. A framework for assessing the degree of acculturation between family members is useful for understanding some the dilemmas faced during cross-cultural transition (Grieger & Ponterotto, 1995). Whether or not counseling programs are accessible to family members of international students is a matter of policy development. If it is beyond the mandate of campus-based services, counselors are in a position to assist with referral and linkage to resources in the local community.

3.4   THE   INTERRELATIONSHIP   BETWEEN COMMON ISSUES OF ADJUSTMENT

A review of the issues commonly faced by international students during cross-cultural transition shows many overlapping and interdependent themes. Although students may be focused on academic achievement, it is difficult to separate academic issues from many other issues of adjustment. For example, the connections between academic abilities, communication, and social support appear to be interwoven for adaptation in the host culture. At the same time, the welfare of family members can be important for maintaining ties of important social support or be a major distraction from academic achievement. What emerges is a pattern of interrelated demands that must be considered in light of competing stressors and sources of personal and academic support. A primary goal of academic achievement means that stability in academic matters is a central concern during cross-cultural transition. Interpersonal relationships are also important for international students in terms of the support that is generated for academic success. There are strong indications that facilitating contact between international students and members of the host culture is crucial for the academic and social success of international students (Westwood & Barker, 1990).

International students obviously need time to adjust themselves to conditions in the host culture. Unfortunately their need for a "slow start" may not parallel the conditions of the host culture and demands for immediate role competency. In the early stages of an academic program, international students are typically in "survival mode" responding in the best ways they know. This can be challenging when some of their usual support systems and resources are not available to them in the host culture. Early pressures for cultural adaptation can lead to faulted decisions and poor judgments that are costly for the student's personal and academic adjustment in the longer term (Westwood & Barker, 1990).

Ironically, the focus on academic demands may prevent students from participating in programming that is intended to support their academic success (Bontrager, Birch, & Kracht, 1990). As students attempt to manage the confusion associated with new academic and community environments, they may be reticent about taking time to participate in campus programs. However, without intervention, the transition issues discussed in this chapter can be serious impediments to the attainment of educational and personal goals. The press for academic success can be mistaken as indifference by others and consequently add to the isolation from available campus support. Counselors must be persistent in reaching out to international students to take advantage of programs that are designed to foster support and ease academic adjustment (Wan et al., 1992). Language support, study skills, and cross-cultural orientations are important services that can be offered in a group format. For specific matters of personal adjustment, individual counseling is an essential service for assisting international students to manage the demands of cross-cultural transition.

4

Re-Entry Transition

4. THE TRANSITION FROM HOST TO HOME CULTURES

Most of the research and programming directed at international student focuses on the initial adjustment to living and learning in a foreign country. However, their transition experiences do not end with the completion of their academic program. The re-entry transition poses particular challenges for international students as they prepare to transfer new personal and educational learning to their home country.

Re-entry is defined as the reacculturation of the individual to the home culture after an extended period of exposure to another culture (Adler, 1981). There are several differences between the transition process of entering a foreign culture and re-entering the home culture (Martin, 1984). One key distinction pertains to expectations. Most international students entering a new culture expect to have difficulties but many of the difficulties of adjustment during re-entry are unexpected (Martin & Harrell, 1996). Along with the personal expectancy for transition issues to occur, other people also expect international students to experience some difficulties. Therefore, members of the host culture may be more tolerant, at least initially, of behavior that is different from their own. In contrast, international students are unlikely to expect to experience difficulties in the transition home and their families and friends may operate with the assumption that international students will "come home the same way" as they left. Neither international students nor their support system at home may be prepared for any re-entry difficulties. A lack of appreciation for the degree of change that occurs during cross-cultural transition increases the risk of adjustment problems and "reverse culture shock" (Gaw, 2000). Some research accounts for the impact of nationality on cross-cultural transitions (Brabant et al., 1990; Martin & Harrell, 1996). It is generally believed that contrasts between the home and host cultures lead to variable re-entry experiences.

A second distinction between the entry and re-entry stages of transition focuses on change (Martin, 1984). Upon entering the foreign culture, international students are more likely to experience predominant changes in the environment. Over time, through exposure to new ways of responding to perceived demands in the new environment, international students internalize change. This subtle process of internal change may only be apparent when the individual returns to the home environment. It is not just the amount of change that occurs that impacts re-entry. The third distinguishing characteristic between the initial and re-entry transition is gaining personal awareness of change (Adler, 1981). It may only be upon returning home that international students, through their own observations or through feedback from family and friends, become aware of the extent to which they have changed through crossing cultures. Higher levels of reverse culture shock are associated with more personal adjustment problems (Gaw, 2000).

Re-entry adjustment may be compounded by the lack of programming to assist international students with their transition home (Westwood, Lawrence, & Paul, 1986). Although most educational institutions that host international students now commonly provide orientation for students upon arrival, services need to address the transition home. It is important for international students to be briefed about the re-entry process in order to consider matters of adjustment before leaving the host culture. This type of "cultural inoculation" serves as a natural extension of earlier programming and assists students to put closures on their experiences in the host country (Arthur, in press; Westwood et al., 1986). This chapter focuses on the re-entry transition and ways that counselors can help students to prepare for returning home.

4.1   The Nature of Re-Entry Transition

The transition experience for international students does not end abruptly at the time they leave the foreign country. It should also not be assumed that reentry begins when international students physically return to their home country. Rather, the nature of re-entry transition is better demarcated as a psychological process than a physical relocation. The reentry transition begins when the international student is still in the foreign country and begins to anticipate returning home. There may be mixed feelings regarding the ending of the foreign experience ranging from euphoria about reuniting with family and friends to a strong desire to remain in the host country. It would seem logical that that the international student's desire to return home would be related to the stress experienced in the re-entry process, however, there is a lack of research to confirm this relationship (Martin, 1984).

Alternatively, the experience of reentry transition may be delayed until some time after the return home. In the latter case, some international students may cope by hanging on to ways of behaving in the foreign culture. This occurs out of preference for new cultural ways, to maintain new forms of behavior, or to avoid or rebel against the realities of life at home (Adler, 1981). These examples of reactive styles for coping with reentry underscore the need for re-entry transition to be defined by internal processes rather than external boundaries of time and place (Martin, 1984). A key point is for counselors to consider the reentry transition within the context of the entire cross-cultural experience (Martin & Harrell, 1996; LaBrack, 1993).

4.1.1   Returning to a "New" Culture

Experience gained as an international student continues to have an impact after returning home. International students enter another period of cultural transition as they face discrepancy between their personal learning and the degree of change in their relationships and other living conditions in their home countries. For some students, foreign education results in a clearer commitment to values in their home culture. For other international students, learning about alternate cultural values prompts dissonance about returning home (Arthur, 1997; Uehara, 1986). Another conceptual approach views reentry as culture learning (Church, 1982; Martin, 1984). Based upon a social learning perspective, it is suggested that the home culture be viewed not as an "old" familiar culture, rather as a "new" culture. It is beneficial for international students to realize that when they return home they may lack reinforcements for behavior and values developed in the host country. Students can be encouraged to seek out and develop new reinforcements and sources of validation, just as they did during their time in the foreign culture.

4.2   Re-Entry Transition Issues

After the duration of their academic program, international students must manage the transition of going home. A common fallacy is that because the student is returning home, there are no obstacles to overcome. However, changes in either the individual or the environment at home can lead to many potential difficulties in the re-entry transition (Martin, 1984). For many students, the months prior to returning home are filled with excitement and anticipation about reunification with friends and family. Feelings of euphoria can overshadow the need to reflect about expectations and to prepare for the transition home (Adler, 1981; Rogers & Ward, 1993). For other students, the end of time in the foreign country is filled with apprehension and uncertainties about returning to life in their home country.

Depending upon the degree of acculturation to the norms and customs of the host country, international students may experience profound changes. However, because the process of change during cross-cultural transition occurs subtly over time, it may only be during re-entry that individuals become aware of the degree to which they have altered their fundamental values and behaviors (Uehara, 1986; Westwood et al., 1986). It may only become apparent when the individual returns home. At that time, conditions in the home country and feedback from significant others frequently provides a mirror to the individual regarding the impact of their foreign education and living experiences. Through the experience of cross-cultural transition, individuals can profoundly change their conceptions of themselves (Wang, 1997). However, it can also be confusing for people to integrate previous notions of identity and the "old self" with shifts in thinking about the world around them and the "new self".

Large discrepancies between expectations and experience increase the likelihood of psychological adjustment problems. When re-entry experiences are more difficult than originally anticipated, students experience greater psychological distress (Gaw, 2000). "If we consider reverse culture shock as a reaction to the cumulative changes in self and home during the sojourner's absence, it is not so surprising that recovering from reentry often takes much longer than the sojourn itself" (Wang, 1997, p. 116). Psychological well-being is enhanced when re-entry experiences are largely more positive than anticipated (Rogers & Ward, 1993). International students have reported concerns about the loss of the host culture, transfer of educational, technical and language expertise, career mobility, conditions in their homeland, and fitting back into existing family, educational, or employment roles (Brabant, Palmer, & Gramling, 1990; Martin & Harrell, 1996; Pedersen, 1990). Issues that emerge during the re-entry transition may prompt international students to question whether or not they will ever feel at home again.

4.3   Leaving the Host Culture to Return Home

The majority of the literature on re-entry transition focuses on the individual's experience upon returning home. However, the re-entry transition entails leaving one culture and returning to another. The experience of making the transition away from the host culture should not be minimized. Even though the terms of becoming an international student imply temporary residence in the host country and inevitably returning home, leaving the host country can be experienced as a profound sense of permanent loss (Wang, 1997). Particularly when there is prolonged exposure to the host culture, international students develop a sense of attachment and belonging. Conflict about where to live after graduation may culminate at the end of an academic program. This issue can be of concern to international students throughout their program and impact the types of decisions made regarding both academic and lifestyle choices (Thomas & Althen, 1989; Walker, 1999).

The re-entry transition represents upheaval or termination to relationships, daily routines, and the student role. Access to material or natural resources and general lifestyle factors may be missed. Aspects of the host culture that were difficult initially can become points of mastery and pride. During re-entry, international students feel like they are leaving behind important personal experiences. Anticipation about returning home may coincide with a sense of loss about leaving those aspects of the host culture behind (Arthur, 1997). International students may feel that leaving the host culture represents leaving parts of themselves behind.

4.4   Social Adjustment

Interaction with family and friends is a critical dimension of re-entry transition. It is primarily through social interaction that international students perceive the changes that have occurred. As a result of exposure to new cultural learning, international students re-enter social relationships in the home environment with a potentially altered "meaning structure", including rules for social interaction (Martin, 1986, p. 4). "Role shock", experienced as confusion and difficulty in relationships with friends and family, may result from changed schemata regarding social interaction. The internalization of new meanings may prompt international students to interpret old symbols and rules differently. This can lead to dissonance about standards of behavior in interpersonal relationships. For example, shifts in the relative freedom prescribed to gender role behavior can be perceived as either restraining or liberating during cross-cultural transitions. Upon returning home, international students may not receive affirmation for new ways of relating. In cases where new behavior strongly contradicts local norms for behavior, there may be strong pressure exerted for adherence. This may be especially true in matters pertaining to intergenerational issues and following established lines of communication and authority (Arthur, 1998).

Perhaps one of the most discouraging realizations for individuals comes from the lack of interest shown by others regarding their cross-cultural experiences. International students may have a greater need to tell loved ones about their experiences than their family and friends have the capacity for listening and understanding (Wang, 1997). As a result, international students miss the commonality of experiences with others in the host country. The availability of close personal relationships in which interest is expressed about the international student's experience has been associated with positive indicators of relationship changes (Martin, 1986). Lack of social support to share experiences and to receive personal validation leads to a sense of isolation during re-entry transition.

In addition to the personal changes that have occurred through the experience of being an international student, family and friends may also have undergone changes. This requires international students to be prepared for the possibility of change in social relationships. It should not be assumed that all relationships will be of equal importance nor will change be uniformly experienced as problematic in all relationships. For example, relationships with parents and siblings have more stability and are more resilient to change than relationships with romantic others and friends (Martin, 1986). Counselors are cautioned against considering change as having entirely positive or negative effects on international student relationships during re-entry. Rather, it is more likely that relationships will be experienced as containing some aspects of both positive and negative change.

4.5   Re-Entry and Gender Issues

In addition to the initial transition issues in the foreign culture, gender role expectations also influence the re-entry process. Similar to the discussion on gender issues in Chapter 3, the research on gender and re-entry suggest that females perceive greater difficulties with both family and daily life (Brabant, Palmer & Gramling, 1990; Wang, 1997). This may be accounted for by the stability of expectations for gender role behavior. In the case of males, family norms often include greater degrees of freedom and opportunities to try out accompanying responsibilities. Norms for male behavior may not fundamentally alter in the transition of living in different countries. However, for females, the stability of family expectations may not match the variability of experiences with gender role behavior. Particularly when female international students come from homes in which traditional values protect females through placing restrictions on the types of relationships and capacity for decision-making, opportunities for trying out new role behavior may be welcomed. However, it is when female international students are expected to return to traditional ways of behavior that gender may be problematic. Lack of privacy, supervision of behavior, and value conflicts in the family are re-entry concerns for female international students.

4.6   Changes in the Home Environment

The focus of re-entry transition is often placed on changes within the individual. However, changes also occur in the home environment. Students who have been able to afford to make visits home find it easier to accommodate physical or social changes in the environment (Brabant et al., 1990). Students who are not in the position to return home until the end of their studies may find abrupt change to be shocking. For example, one international student was unable to afford to fly home upon learning about the death of his mother. Apart from dealing with the grief over his personal loss at the time of learning about her death, his anticipation about going home was profoundly affected. This was stated as, "I can't imagine what life at home will be without my mother." For other students, changes in the home environment may be on a larger scale, related to economic or political influences. This is exemplified in the experiences of students who study overseas while their country is engaged in war. There may be apprehension about returning home when requirements for military service are in effect, facing the loss of family and friends killed in the war, or concerns about conflict between former neighbors and friends. Natural disasters such as floods or draught impact the local environment. Recent economic fluctuations in markets around the world have substantially impact the standard of living in many nations. Vast fluctuations in economic power, including inflation and higher costs of living, can lead to dramatic contrasts between the quality of lifestyle afforded prior to and following foreign studies.

Another possibility exists that the environment remains relatively static during the period of foreign education. What international students notice about life at home is salient. Individual perceptions determine what is experienced as stressful during transitions (Lazarus & Folkman, 1984). For example, what was taken for granted in the past as "the way things are" may be noticed upon re-entry. Exposure to contrasting ideas leads students to view cultural practices in their home country with either new appreciation or with a critical view (Uehara, 1986). This can occur on many levels, ranging from interactions with family or friend to macro levels pertaining to political or social policies (Martin, 1984). Faced with contrasting ways in which social systems are organized, international students gain different views of local and global practices (Uehara, 1986). The experience of living and learning in a foreign country can lead to consciousness-raising on many levels.

4.6.1   Change Has Reciprocal Influences

As a general rule, it is the relative difference between changes within the individual and the environment that facilitates re-entry adaptation (Martin, 1986). This qualification points out that some changes in the environment may be compatible with personal learning and actually ease the reentry transition. This occurs when socio-economic conditions improve in countries or norms for behavior become more flexible. Alternatively, when exposure to a new culture results in an affirmation and valuing of traditional ways, the re-entry home provides relief to be in the comfort of familiar practices. Adjustment issues are triggered when international students experience a high degree of assimilation to new ways of behaving and become accustomed to accessing available resources in the foreign environment. Where change has not occurred at such a rapid pace or in similar directions as the foreign culture, international students may particularly feel that they no longer "fit in". It is the lack of change in the home environment that results in frustration upon re-entry. When international students have undergone considerable internal changes, returning to a static environment may lead to severe problems of adjustment.

4.7   Career Concerns

Surprisingly, there has been little written about the career development needs of international students. In one needs assessment, international students wanted work experience, interviewing strategies, and job search skills (Spencer-Rodgers, 2000). Job search clubs for international students can influence competencies such as career self-efficacy, career decision-making, and help to consolidate vocational identity (Bikos & Furry, 1999). Career development variables such as vocational identity, developing a stable understanding of aspirations, interests, and abilities, may be impacted by international students' acculturation level (Shih & Brown, 2000). The scope of research on international students' career concerns needs to expand to a comprehensive view of career transition. International students require career and life planning skills (Mori, 2000). From the point of arriving in the host country, students should be preparing for their eventual return home, including future academic and occupational plans (NAFSA, 1996).

For the majority of international students, their motives to study abroad are inextricably linked to the enhancement of their professional expertise. Foreign education is typically pursued to gain exposure to the curriculum and culture of the host country. The choice to study abroad, enrolling in post-secondary education, selecting an academic program, and academic success are key career-related factors in the early stages of transition. However, other issues become salient for the career development of international students during the re-entry process. At the time when returning graduates must manage reverse culture shock and shifting roles and expectations, they are also faced with the challenge of transferring their foreign education into the local setting.

Individuals who are continuing in the student role often find large disparities between the curriculum of host and home countries. This can prompt another period of adjustment to the teaching methodology used in local schools. For those international students who have completed their education, re-entry may entail transition into the local work force. In either circumstance, the potential loss or decay of skills is a major concern. This includes general skills such as language, or specific skills relevant to their occupational choice. Lack of opportunity to implement and practice skills acquired in the host country leads to loss of expertise.

4.7.1   Integrating International Experience

Another career development issue faced by returning international students is the suitability of occupational placements (Pedersen, 1990). This may occur either because work settings in the home country lack comparable resources, i.e., equipment, technical facilities, work systems, that the international student has gained expertise in using. As a result, this may make it difficult to translate theoretical knowledge gained through international education to practical applications. Another factor is the lack of contact of occupational information supplied to international students during their studies abroad. Few embassies or their educational attaches apprise students who are studying in other countries of employment opportunities in their own countries (Pedersen, 1990).

Beyond the availability of resources lies a larger issue of organizational career development. Many organizations are simply unprepared for employees who have gained international expertise and are uninformed about how to facilitate their career development (Arthur, 2002). Co-workers who have not had the same opportunities and who are less motivated for organizational change are often hostile towards new ways of working. Consequently, the returning international student may face unsatisfactory work arrangements that contribute to dissatisfaction (Martin & Harrell, 1996. These are barriers that prevent international students from using international expertise in their worker role. In contrast, organizations that have taken an active role in sponsorship and who have developed a strategy for integrating international students may capitalize upon their expertise. In these cases, students who are successful in obtaining employment sponsorship have considerable advantages upon returning home. This is true for students from less developed countries where opportunities are greater because fewer professionals have international education (Pedersen, 1990). For many international students, foreign expertise provides opportunities to be leaders in their chosen occupational field.

4.8   Preparing International Students for the Re-Entry Transition

Counseling interventions for the re-entry transition is a natural extension of orientation programming offered to international students during their entry transition (LaBrack, 1993). Re-entry programming assists students with the closure experience of leaving the host country, help them to integrate their experiences, and encourages them to consider life at home. International students may not see the need for re-entry assistance, particularly those students who have not considered that their move home may trigger another stage of cross-cultural transition. As mentioned earlier in this chapter, people frequently underestimate the degree of adjustment that they fact when returning to their home culture and are not prepared for another experience of culture shock. Re-entry programming is intended to educate students about this stage of cross-cultural transition, as a form of "cultural inoculation" to prepare for life at home. There are four underlying goals of interventions designed to address the re-entry transition, (a) convincing participants that reverse culture shock is real, that it affects every returning sojourner to some degree, and that it usually goes unrecognized; (b) encouraging participants to think about changes in themselves, changes at home, and what effect those changes are going to have on their reentry experience; (c) suggesting that participants start worrying about their return; and (d) convincing participants that there are measures they can take to assure that their own reentry is *relatively* painless in the short run, and a positive growth experience in the long run" (Wang, 1997, p.110).

4.9   Psychoeducational   Approaches   to   Re-Entry Programming

A group approach, in the form of a psychoeducational workshop can be used to introduce re-entry issues. A re-entry workshop is a cost-effective way for counselors to connect with students and opens the door for them to make contact for individual counselling, if required (Arthur, in press). There are other advantages to a group approach in the delivery of counselling services. For example, international students benefit from hearing from their peers about potential re-entry demands that they had not previously considered. Group interaction stimulates affective experiences that prompt new learning or reframing of issues pertaining to the re-entry transition (Wang, 1997; Westwood et al., 1986). It is also beneficial for international students to share strategies for managing re-entry transition concerns. The group is also a valuable resource for generating ideas and resources about the transition home.

In developing a re-entry workshop for international students, counselors should keep three goals in mind (Arthur, in press). First, international students should be given an opportunity to reflect upon their experiences of living and learning in the host country. Debriefing of student sharing should focus on the process of cross-cultural transition. This is a starting place for students to consider, a) how much they have changed, b) their academic and personal accomplishments, c) areas of impending loss as they leave the host country, and d) the coping strategies that helped them manage transition demands. This sets the stage for the second goal of a re-entry workshop, in which students are encouraged to reflect about returning home. Discussion can focus on students' hopes and fears, positive aspects and any concerns that they have about returning home. It is helpful for the counsellor facilitator of the workshop to introduce the re-entry home, not as returning to a familiar place, but as the "new" culture that they are entering (Martin, 1984). This helps students to appreciate that they may confront change, in themselves, in their relationships, or in their surroundings. Debriefing supports students to work with general thoughts or feelings about going home and to define specific issues and problem-solving strategies (Westwood et al., 1986).

4.9.1   Critical Incidents

Counselors can structure re-entry workshops in a way that provides international students with core information about re-entry transitions, while leaving time for open-ended discussion between participants. The use of critical incidents in teaching methodology supports the goals of a re-entry workshop (Arthur, in press). There are two types critical incidents that can be incorporated in workshop planning. First, critical incidents can be probed through a process of structured inquiry focused on key area of transition, i.e., new learning in the host country, adjustment difficulties, local customs, personal learning, appreciations about home culture, concerns about returning home. In designing these types of critical incident probes, the goal is to help students focus on vivid events that people consider to be meaningful and significant in their experience as a learner (Brookfield, 1995). Focused prompts provide structure while supporting the experiences of individuals to be shared and compared.

A second type of critical incidents involves the use of prepared vignettes, based on the prior experiences of international students. Vignettes provide workshop participants with some background information through the use of scenarios. They can help international students to consider specific issues and generate discussion about problem-solving strategies. Counselors can design vignettes, based upon the themes that are uncovered from the first type of critical incident, or from their prior experiences counselling international students. It is also helpful to include other members of a student services team, such as an international student advisor, to gather input about the perceived needs of international students during re-entry programming.

4.9.2   Central Messages

A re-entry workshop helps student services staff, including counselors, to become better informed about the transition issues and coping strategies used by international students. What surfaces in a re-entry workshop captures many of the highlights of living and learning in the host culture. This is valuable information for future program planning. It can also give student services staff an indication of how students represent their experiences. The best ambassadors for any educational institutions are student consumers who tell others about their positive experiences with academic and support services at the school they attended. Finally, a re-entry workshop is one of the last points of contact with international students before they depart for home. A strong message of "we care about what will happen to you" is a wonderful sendoff for students returning home. Counselors have an important role in helping students integrate their experiences of living and learning in a foreign culture and preparing for the re-entry transition home.

4.10   Taking International Experience Home

A wide range of issues may arise in the transition experiences of international students. It is worth remembering that not all students will have difficulties with the same issues neither will their experiences necessarily lead to problematic personal or academic adjustment. Students are likely to have a range of expectations and both positive and negative experiences in the re-entry process (Brabant et al., 1990; Uehara, 1986). Although there is more research available that attests to the adjustment concerns at the point of entering the new culture, the existing studies suggest that the transition home can be equally, if not more, difficult.

Having made the point about individual differences, however, it remains clear that preparing international students for the issues that they may encounter during cross-cultural transitions is an important preventive strategy. Through preparing international students to consider possible events in their re-entry transition, a process of sensitization to their actual experience begins (Westwood et al., 1986). Anticipatory coping may assist international students to manage the realities they will face at home.

There is a paucity of research investigating the long-term benefits and growth that can accompany international students on their journey home. "Reverse culture shock ... may be considered a long-term process of coming to terms with oneself as amore complex, more multicultural individual in a changed but familiar setting" (Wang, 1997, p. 116). Programs designed to address re-entry issues can assist international students to consider both short- and long-terms aspects of their experience. Beyond identifying possible difficulties in the re-entry transition, programs can also facilitate discovery of cultural and personal learning. Re-entry preparation is a prerequisite in programming for international students in order to maximize the benefits of studying abroad and to minimize the problems of adjustment in the transition home (Westwood et al., 1986). Clearly, the responsibility for re-entry programming lies with the host institution. Considering the investment made in international education and the importance of students returning home with a favorable impression of the host institution, re-entry programming takes relatively small effort and can yield big advantages. As one of the last contact points with an educational institution, re-entry programming goes a long way in sending home with students a clear message of support and concern for their future.

5

Multicultural Counseling Competencies for Working with International Students

5. COUNSELING INTERNATIONAL STUDENTS ACROSS CULTURES

Counseling international students inevitably involves counseling across cultures. Even in the rare cases where counselors are from the same country as international students, it should not be assumed that their worldviews are similar. It should also not be assumed that because clients are international students, that they will experience problems of adjustment that require counseling intervention. Defining any group according to specific characteristics can lead to assumptions about counseling issues and appropriate interventions. Consequently, counselors require a repertoire of multicultural competencies for working with international students (Arthur, 1997; Sue & Sundberg, 1996). Multicultural counseling competencies help counselors to consider the commonalties between students who are culturally diverse while at the same time respecting the unique circumstances and counseling needs of individual students.

5.1   Universal and Culture-Specific Perspectives

In the counseling literature, there is debate about the advantages and disadvantages of targeting groups on the basis of specific cultural variables, i.e., gender, ethnicity, race, age, ability, sexual orientation, socio-economic status. Some argue that defining multicultural populations on the basis of specific cultural variables risks stereotyping clients and perpetuating their marginalization (Arthur & Stewart, 2001; Sue et al., 1998). Counselors must be cautious about assuming that the needs of people from specific cultural groups are uniform. This same argument can be applied to perceptions about international students. Viewing international students only on the group level risks homogenizing their experiences and ignoring the tremendous cultural variability within this student population (Pedersen, 1991; Popadiuk &

Arthur, in press). The voices and experiences of individual students may not be heard by counselors who adopt a general approach in understanding the experiences of international learners. Unfortunately, this risks further marginalization of international students as they are seen as a "separate population" on campus. Inter-cultural variability also needs to be taken into account in the design and delivery of counseling services (Popadiuk & Arthur, in press).

Knowing that a client is an international student provides counselors with very little information about how to proceed. Rather than utilizing group membership as a classifying variable to determine client needs a generic approach to multicultural counseling offers an alternative point of view. Advocates of this position consider every encounter with a client as a cross-cultural exchange, in that there are relative similarities and differences between the worldviews of counselors and clients (Pedersen, 2001; Weinrach & Thomas, 1996). This position underscores the need for counselors to consider the worldview and unique counseling issues of each international student. Counselor are challenged to adopt a "culture-centered" perspective (Pedersen & Ivey, 1993) in which the influences of the larger society are considered along with the particular worldview of the client. This does not eliminate the need for counselors to examine the salience of cultural characteristics such as race, gender, or religion for international student's experience. Issues of racism, sexism, or homophobia continue to permeate the attitudes and behavior of individuals, including counselors, and are reflected in the policies and practices of organizations (Helms, 1994, Sue et al., 1998). Although counselors are generally familiar with their roles in individual or group counseling, they can also play a major role in promoting social equity. In educational institutions, this means working to improve the climate for culturally diverse learners, including policies, procedures in service delivery and the responsiveness of staff towards international students. To assist counselors in developing culturally responsive services, this chapter is devoted to multicultural counseling competencies, with special attention to applications with international students.

5.2   Multicultural Counseling Competencies

The counseling profession has identified the need for counselor education programs to support students for their professional roles with culturally diverse clients. In response, members of the Division of Counseling Psychology (Division 17) of the American Psychological Association formed a committee for the purpose of developing culturally relevant counseling competencies (Sue et al., 1998). This proactive work in the United States, 25 years ago, has changed the ways that we think about counselor education in North America. Competencies resulting from this initiative were published in The Counseling Psychologist (Sue et al., 1982) and the revised competencies were jointly published 10 years later in the *Journal for Multicultural Counseling and Development* and the *Journal for Counseling and Development* (Sue, Arredondo, & McDavis, 1992). Since the publication of these seminal works, the counseling literature has flourished to expand the various dimensions of multicultural counseling competence, e.g., Pedersen & Ivey, 1993; Ponterrotto, Casa, Suzuki, & Alexander, 1995, 2001; Sue et al., 1998; Sue & Sue, 1990, 1999). These landmark publications provide a strong rationale for a multicultural perspective in the counseling profession. They have moved the field past rationales for multicultural counseling competencies to articulating specific standards and competencies that define multicultural counseling competence. These publications serve as a template for students in counselor education programs to define and develop competent professional practices. Experienced counselors can utilize these resources in the design of professional development programs to enhance their repertoire of multicultural counseling competencies. Counselors who work with international students are encouraged to refer directly to these publications as sources to self-assess their current levels of multicultural counseling competencies and to identify potential areas for personal and professional growth. The multicultural competencies provide guidelines towards which to aspire in an ongoing program of professional development. They are also a useful compliment to professional codes of ethics in that they specify ways in which counselors can improve their competencies for ethical practice with clients who are culturally diverse.

Multicultural counseling competencies have been defined in three major domains: Self-awareness, knowledge, and skills. Self-awareness competencies refer to counselors' understanding about how their personal cultural background potentially impacts professional practice. Knowledge competencies focus on counselors' understanding of the background, history, and current socialization influences of cultural groups. Skill competencies refer to counselors' capacity to design and delivery culturally-responsive counseling services. Recently, the fourth dimension of organizational development has been addressed as an essential multicultural competence (Sue et al., 1998). In recognition that counseling occurs in a cultural context, policies and practices of organizations are examined in light of client access and potential barriers. In the following sections of this chapter, each domain of the multicultural counseling competencies will be expanded upon, using examples to highlight the application of multicultural counseling competencies with international students.

5.3   Multicultural   Counseling   Competencies: Self-Awareness

Self-awareness is the foundation of multicultural counseling competence. Counselors should think about developing self-awareness, not as an end state, but as an ongoing process. This includes continuous reflection about the potential influences of personal culture on one's professional role as a counselor. Some people have argued that one's personal life can be separated from one's work role. This appears like an impossible task, as values, beliefs, feelings, and experiences with people culminate together to form our worldview. It is untenable that our impressions about culture can be turned on an off, according to the roles we hold in life. It is human nature to form perceptual schemata around culture, and our core beliefs strongly come into play in novel or ambiguous situations (Ridley, Mendoza, Kanitz, Angermeier, & Zenk, 1994; Lazarus & Folkman, 1984). Counselors who work with international students are not immune to images of this population. Their prior experience with people from other cultures can be either an asset or barrier towards delivering responsive services. A key question that counselors need to continually ask is, "How does my prior experience impact how I work with this international student?" Our perceptual schemas are based on prior experiences, including how information about international students is received, screened, and interpreted. One of the main goals of promoting greater self-awareness in multicultural counseling competencies is to help counselors increase their cultural sensitivity. This is defined as "the ability of counselors to acquire, develop, and actively use an accurate cultural perceptual schema in the course of multicultural counseling" (Ridley et al., 1994). This ability is related to the capacity of counselors for cultural empathy (Ridley & Lingle, 1996) or whether ethnocentric views of clients and their issues detracts from cultural empathy.

5.3.1   Cultural Encapsulation and Unintentional Oppression

The importance of self-awareness is related to cultural encapsulation. This refers to people's tendency to see the world through one set of assumptions based upon their own self-referenced experience (Wrenn, 1962). Culturally encapsulated counselors judge international students on the basis of prior experience people who remind them of the student, see their problems through their own definition of the situation, and impose interventions that are based upon their notions of helpfulness. Even counselors with the best of intentions in mind and who welcome the opportunity to work with international students can introduce cultural bias into the counseling process in ways that are inadvertently harmful. The expression of encapsulation may be unintentional (Pedersen, 1995; Ridley, 1995) in that counselors are unaware of how their cultural biases add dimensions of oppression to the experiences of clients. The following examples illustrate some of the ways that unintentional oppression may be introduced to counseling practices with international students.

5.3.1.1 Cultural Blindness

In this scenario, counselors adapt the stance that "everyone is equal" and operate from a belief system underpinned by the axiom, "Treat others as you would like to have them treat you." In the name of equity, counselors inadvertently may contribute to the veil of silence about difficult issues such as racism and sexism. Unfortunately, as outlined in Chapter 3, discrimination continues to be a reality in the experiences of many international students. Ignoring the potential influences of social differences, counselors act as if these do not exist in our society. Adopting a position of cultural blindness allows counselors to avoid dealing with their own biases or acknowledging their privilege (Helms, 1994; McIntosh, 1988, 1998) at the expense of ignoring or overlooking real issues in the lives of international students. Treating others as you would like to be treated keeps counseling centered in the preferences of the counselor as opposed to taking a hard look at what is needed and what would work best from the point of view of an international student client.

In discussing issues of oppression with students and with counselors, part of the barrier may be a reluctance to bring forward difficult issues such as racism, socioeconomic status, or issues of sexual orientation. Out of fears of offending clients or introducing content that might not be the client's agenda, counselors chose to avoid talking about cultural dimensions, or assessing their salience for the client. Counselors often wait for the client to introduce topics pertaining to culture, with the assumption, "if it is important, the client will bring it up". This position places the onus on international students to bring forward issues that may be ambiguous, often at a time in their life where they are facing a considerable amount of personal disruption, in a new context, and in a professional relationship that they lack experience. International students may also lack confidence about initiating conversations about culture, for fear of being judged, or for fear of not being validated. The result is a counselor and a client attempting to work together without addressing important issues of culture.

5.3.1.2 Shining the Cultural Spotlight

In this scenario, counselors overemphasize cultural dimensions. Client issues are squeezed into problems of culture, versus considering the potential influences of culture as a tentative hypothesis for understanding client concerns. The adage, "if you have a hammer, everything looks like a nail," applies here. Counselors who work with international students must guard against making assumptions about the basis of clients' concerns. Although it is prudent to assess for the ways that culture intersects with client concerns, making culture *the issue* risks offending clients. For example, international students face many of the same adjustment demands as local students (Arthur, 1997). When they approach a counselor to talk about academic issues, counselors must address the presenting issue and open the door to talk about other potential transition issues. It should not be assumed that something "deeper" is the real counseling agenda. As one international student expressed, "All I wanted to do was talk about my problem with writing tests, and the counselor kept making it out as something bigger than that." Out of concern for incorporating culture into their practices with international students, counselors must be careful about going overboard in their eagerness to incorporate culture; counselors will miss seeing the individual and the issues of importance.

5.3.1.3 Minimizing Culture Shock in Counseling

In chapter 2, culture shock was the primarily construct used to explain the reaction of people faced with cultural contrasts. It is generally believed that the severity of culture shock is determined by the degree of similarity or difference between the culture of origin and the new culture (Pedersen, 1991). However, little has been written about the potential for culture shock in professional relationships when two people with fundamentally different worldviews meet together. Counselors or clients may experience a reaction, akin to culture shock, when their usual ways of communicating with others are less effective, when they struggle to find common ground, and when the usual cues for interpreting behavioral cues are confusing or inaccurate. This is not an unusual experience in counseling international students. Coupled with the fact that many international students do not have prior experience with counseling, they may even break cultural norms about how to behave as clients!

The cognitive dissonance and emotional discomfort that is triggered for counselors in their work with culturally diverse clients needs to be recognized. This experience of culture shock may be settled by counselors through retreating to a position of cultural encapsulation (Achenbach & Arthur, 2002). In order to end their discomfort about the difficulties of working with an international student, whose presentation does not conform to their expectations, counselors may impose their personal views about the client. It is easy for labels such as "difficult" or "defensive" to be placed upon the client, when, in fact, it may be the counsellor's difficulty in working across cultures that is creating tension in the counseling interview. Unfortunately, counselors who have a difficult interaction with an international student may filter that experience as a generalization about all international students.   Alternatively, counselors can learn to use their metacognitive skills to pay attention to their emotional reactions when working with international students.   If they can suspend their need for self-protection and use their emotional reaction of culture shock as a guide, they can move forward into a position of learning together with the client. This is a prime time to be reflective about, "What does this mean about the culture of the client?"   It is imperative that counselors take this reflection one step further and ask, "What does this mean about my personal culture?" Counselors need to adjust their expectations about standards for appropriate client behavior and how a therapeutic encounter should unfold (Leong & Chou, 1996; Pedersen, 1995).   Counselors who work with international students can build their multicultural competencies of self-awareness through a willingness to recognize when they are turning away from cultural differences.   They can embrace those differences as a challenge to find common ground to build an effective working alliance.   Working across cultures requires counselors to engage in a learning process about others and about themselves.

5.4   Multicultural Counseling Competencies: Knowledge

The essence of the multicultural counseling domain of knowledge is to gain background information in order to understand and appreciate clients' worldviews. In order to move beyond a position of cultural encapsulation, counselors need to become knowledgeable about the history, values, and contemporary issues impacting the client groups that are consumers of counseling services.   The multicultural counseling competencies of self-awareness and knowledge have reciprocal influences.   It is only through gaining familiarity with another culture, that one can appreciate the uniqueness of one's personal culture.   Likewise, awareness about personal culture can help counselors to appreciate both the commonalities and differences likely to be encountered in working with clients from diverse cultures. Most professional codes of ethics, i.e., American Psychological Association, 1995; Canadian Psychological Association, 1996, contain general guidelines regarding competencies for working with culturally diverse populations.   Some professional codes offer specialist guidelines that emphasize the importance of competence for working with clients in a non-discriminatory manner, i.e., Canadian Psychological Association, 1996; NAFSA: Association of International Educators (1992) has developed a code of ethics that is relevant for all members of educational institutions who work with international students.

5.4.1   Increasing Knowledge about International Students

Counselors can increase their knowledge about international students through several avenues. They can access professional publications that are written specifically for professionals who are educators and who work in student services positions with international students. Organizations such as the Association of Universities and Colleges of Canada www.aucc.ca, the Canadian Bureau of International Education http://www/cbie.ca, the Institute of International Education, and NAFSA: Association of International Educators http://www.nafsa.org, develop materials pertaining to international students, including research publications, resources online, and newsletters for use by staff and students. Professional journals in the counseling, education, and student services fields are publishing more articles pertaining to international students. The types of articles, including empirically based questionnaire research with international students, are expanding to include qualitative research studies and articles written from the perspectives of international students (Popadiuk & Arthur, in press). These are useful sources to enhance knowledge about international students.

5.4.1.1 Culture-Specific Knowledge

Counselors can go beyond the general literature about international students and access sources of culture-specific information. Some opponents of multicultural counseling argue that it is impossible to know everything about every culture. In reply, this seems to be an impossible argument that detracts from what is possible. In order to be culturally sensitive, counselors need to be knowledgeable about the unique experiences of particular cultural groups (Jacob & Greggo, 2001). Counselors can access information about the predominant groups of international students that are enrolled as students on their campuses. Knowledge of enrollment trends is a good step towards knowing who is in the student population, who are potential clients, and considering ways to ease access to counseling services for all students. As the counseling field increasingly recognizes the problems of grouping many cultures into one category, i.e, Asians, increased attention is being paid to specific cultural groups. There is also increasing attention being paid to the intersection of cultural dimensions such as ethnicity and gender, so that the forces of culture within group membership are considered. Counselors may also find it useful to extend their reading outside the professional literature to other sources of media that portray the experiences of people from other cultures.

5.4.1.2 Utilizing Community Resources

Counselors can learn a lot from involvement in multicultural events in their local community. Ties with community leaders and associations in the local community can help counselors to provide external support for international students who newly arrive to a country. Alternatively, counselors may be able to access consultation from the local community to discuss issues pertaining to counseling students who share a similar cultural background.

5.4.1.3 Learning Directly from International Students

There is probably no better source of learning than directly from international students. Counselors' involvement in the international student community on campus will accentuate their knowledge and demonstrate a genuine interest in students. This can be done an informal basis through spending time in the international student center during lunch hours when many students visit the center, joining excursions designed for international students, or participating in events that highlight campus internationalization. Many campuses have student clubs, organized around student ethnicity, in which many international students take part. Again, connection with student leaders can help counselors to gain a wealth of information about the culture. In turn, effort expended by counselors to establish a profile with international students is likely the single most important factor to help students access counseling services in the future. Personal connection with international students helps them to overcome many of the uncertainties about accessing professional services.

5.4.2   Knowledge about Cultural Influences

Beyond culture specific information, counselors need to be aware of the psychological processes that impact culturally diverse learners. Three in particular are identified here as key directions for counselors' knowledge acquisition: acculturation, racial identity, and discrimination.

5.4.2.1 Acculturation Influences

Acculturation was introduced in Chapter 2 as a core concept for understanding the transition experiences of international students (Berry, 1985, 1997). Counselors need to appreciate that the degree of acculturation experienced by an international student changes over time. Some changes are deliberate, when the student intentionally sets out to learn about the host culture, or decides to connect in a stronger ways to the values and norms of the home culture. Other changes may be less deliberate, and by the very nature of exposure and experience interacting with people in the host culture, international students may change more than they ever expected. The extent to which international students acculturate to the host culture may not be fully recognized until the re-entry home (Arthur, in press; Gaw, 2000). Intergenerational conflict and gender role conflict are common sources of stress between international students and their family members and need to be viewed as an outcome of the acculturation process (Baptiste, 1993). Parental expectations for children, even adult children, may be challenged as international students are exposed to new ideas and lifestyle options such as career plans. This can be a particular issue for women students who experience more freedom in gender roles during their time as an international student than what is allowed in their home country. Acculturation issues can surface in many areas of decision-making for international students, and counselors must be careful that their values do not inadvertently influence decisions by students that can have longer-term consequences in their home culture (Arthur, 1998).

5.4.2.2 Incorporating Racial Identity

Racial identity is an area within counseling practice has gained increasing attention as the majority of counselors continue to be from White, European backgrounds (Sue & Sue, 1990). The worldviews of White counselors need to be deconstructed to understand how positions of power and privilege influence interactions with clients who are culturally different (MacIntosh, 1988, 1998; Neville, Worthington, & Spanierman, 2001). Models of White racial identity have been developed with the explicit assumption that racism is tied to socialization and identity development (Helms, 1995; Rowe, Bennett, & Atkinson, 1994; Sue et al., 1998). Counselors who work with international students are bound to work with clients from different racial backgrounds. White counselors can benefit from examining their own process of identity development and from considering how beliefs about racial supremacy may consciously or unconsciously impact their professional practices (Ridley, 1995). Counselors often find this material difficult to work through and they may experience strong feelings ranging from guilt, anger, and shame. However, these feelings can motivate counselors to gain deeper levels of personal awareness and knowledge about how to address issues of race and other forms of oppression with international students.

Knowledge of other models, such as Black (e.g., Cross, 1995; Helms, 1995), Asian (e.g., Lee, 1991; Sue & Sue, 1971) and Latino/Hispanic (e.g., Casas & Pytluk, 1995, Ruiz, 1990) racial and ethnicity identity models, or general models of minority identity development (Atkinson et al., 1989) helps counselors to appreciate the influences of racial identity on educational and personal experiences. Previous research has suggested the relationships between various identity states and levels of psychological adjustment

(Helms, 1986). Racial identity may have an impact on both the adjustment issues of international students and their experiences with counseling (Bagley & Copeland, 1994).

5.4.2.3 Addressing Discrimination

Unfortunately, discrimination continues to be a common experience in the lives of many international students. Counselors need to understand how discrimination can adversely influence the psychological well-being of different cultural groups and the development of individuals. Discrimination is a huge barrier for international students in feeling at home in the host culture, and in devoting energy to their academic studies. As noted in Chapter 3, some international students may, for the first time in their lives, be a racial minority of the host culture. The abrupt realization of racial differences can be alarming for students and influence their social interactions. Some international students are hypervigilant about their visible differences and wonder how this characteristic impacts people's reactions to them. Other students miss peers and role models who share racial similarity. Their separateness from family, friends, and their community is heightened by awareness about racial differences.

The behavior of members of the host culture towards international students can be blatantly or discretely discriminatory. International students already expend considerable energy navigating a foreign culture, often in their second language. It takes an enormous amount of energy to be monitoring their personal behavior for social appropriateness and to screen and interpret the behavior of others. Acts of discrimination can be especially stressful for international students who are uncertain about how to respond in the host culture. It takes enormous courage for international students to bring up issues of discrimination, for fear about how people in authority will perceive them. Counselors must also be comfortable about naming situations and behavior as discriminatory to help international students take appropriate action. In turn, international students must be apprised about codes of conduct for behavior in the local educational context. Including policies about discrimination and harassment in orientation materials informs international students about appropriate behavior, both their own behavior and the behavior of people in the host culture.

5.4.3   Holding Cultural Knowledge in Tentative Ways

A cautionary note is in order developing knowledge competencies for multicultural counseling with international students. The counseling literature on international students provides counselors with many resources to learn about their common issues and experiences. General information, along with culture-specific information, can serve as useful background knowledge.

Counselors need to hold this information in a tentative way, and test out its applicability for understanding the experiences of individual students. Holding general knowledge "loosely" allows counselors to hear the stories of international students, and appreciate the uniqueness of their situations. Counselors need to adopt a position of "learner" in encouraging international students to be the experts about their situation, including the experts about their culture. That is different than expecting international students to teach counselors everything they need to know about international students and their specific culture. The onus is on the counselor to gather background knowledge that supports their multicultural counseling competence for working with international students. Time in sessions should not be wasted with clients educating counselors about basic information that is available through alternate sources. It is valid to explore culture and to clarify the relevance of cultural information for framing clients' issues, however, boundaries need to be drawn about exploiting international students as "cultural teachers." For example, an international student was referred to a counselor for a specific problem he was having with test anxiety. When I asked the student about his experience in counseling, he said, "I went, but please don't expect me to go back. I spent 40 minutes of the session answering the counsellor's questions about my country, and then it was time to go. I really needed help and did not get it." Counselors need to be informed as much as possible, with background knowledge about international students to facilitate an effective working alliance in counseling.

5.5   Multicultural Counseling Competencies: Skills

Counselors who work with international students actively develop and practice intervention strategies and skills that are culturally responsive. A key goal of multicultural counseling skills is to apply methods that are relevant for client needs, and are valued by clients. This may require counselors to step outside their usual ways of practicing. "It is important for counselors working with international students to broaden their understanding of counseling beyond narrowly defined methods and contexts" (Pedersen, 1991, p. 29). This often requires counselors to do things differently than how they were trained in counselor education programs. Ultimately, counselors need to consider how their clients will benefit from their counseling skills. The efficacy of counseling with international students is increased when their counseling issues are defined in ways that are consistent with the life experience of clients and when interventions are valued by clients for their relevance (Sue et al., 1998).

5.5.1   Culturally Responsive Communication Skills

One of the first areas for examination is the use of counseling microskills. Counselors are often taught culturally-bounded communication techniques such as direct eye contact, facing the client, open posture, and direct questions during counseling interviews. Counselors must consider how meanings of communication are interpreted across culture. This includes consideration of verbal communication and nonverbal communication such as proxemics (use of personal and interpersonal space), kinesics (bodily movements), and paralanguage (vocal cues) (Sue & Sue, 1999). Culturally competent counselors are able to tailor their communication skills to help clients feel more comfortable. Counselors also need to be aware of the potential interpretations that can be assigned to communication styles. Counselors assist international students through helping them to understand the nuances of communication in the host culture and potential meanings assigned to their own behavior and the behavior of others.

5.5.1.1 Cognitive Complexity

An important skill for counselors is cognitive complexity (Pedersen & Ivey, 1993). Cognitive complexity allows counselors to consider a number of counseling hypotheses concurrently, including the salience of cultural dimensions for a client's presenting issues. Counselors who hold high levels of cognitive complexity are also able assess the cultural variables that change as the counseling process unfolds, and are able to consider the influences of culture on the therapeutic alliance. There is a strong connection between counselors' cognitive complexity and their tolerance of ambiguity. As noted in the discussion about self-awareness, counselors with low tolerance of ambiguity tend to retreat to ethnocentrism to resolve the situation. It is proposed that counselors with higher levels of cognitive complexity are better able to tolerate ambiguity and simultaneously entertain a number of explanations. This helps counselors to stay engaged with clients to learn about their issues and helps counselors to avoid drawing premature conclusions about clients and about their presenting issues (Arthur & Stewart, 2001).

5.5.2   Multiple Counselor Roles

Multicultural competence requires counselors to examine their professional beliefs about the ways that counselors should work with clients. In addition to clinical roles such as individual or group counseling, counselors need to be skilled to engage in psycheducational or systems intervention roles (Sue et al., 1998). This means expanding a repertoire of skills for working directly with international students, working with people who come into contact with international students, or working with others to examine and revise programs and policies that impact international students. Several of the roles outlined for counseling racial and/or ethnic minorities (Atkinson, Thompson, & Grant, 1993) are relevant for counseling international students.

5.5.2.1 Teaching

Counselors are skilled at instructing international students about what counseling is and how it can support their academic and personal success. Counselors participate in international student workshops for specific topics such as culture shock, coping with transition, or preparing for re-entry. Teaching skills are utilized in campus programming on internationalization to inform other staff members about international students.

5.5.2.2 Advising

Counselors are called upon directly by international students for information and referral to other resources on campus or in the community. Other members of the campus community may consult with counselors about particular issues concerning international students.

5.5.2.3 Consulting

Counselors work together with other members of student services to coordinate or design programming for international student. An extension of the consulting role for counselors is serving as a "cultural consultant" or "cultural broker". Expertise in relationships across cultures can be called upon to help international students develop knowledge and skills for navigating local cultural norms. In turn, members of the campus community may call upon counselors for preparation, problem solving, or mediation in situations of cross-cultural conflict.

5.5.2.4 Advocacy

Another key role for counselors includes advocacy on behalf of international students. Counselors have responsibilities for promoting equitable treatment for international students, which often means addressing systemic or personal biases in the treatment of this student population. Advocacy skills should extend beyond crisis management to include health promotion and prevention roles by working towards a campus environment that is welcoming and supportive for learners.

Counselors' roles for working with international students frequently overlap. In the design of counseling services, it is important to allow time for work that is traditionally the domain of counseling, i.e., individual and group counseling. Time to design and implement outreach activities on campus must be legitimized as important roles for counselors.

5.5.3   Adapting Counseling Interventions

Culturally skilled counselors consider how their training represents particular cultural values, norms and professional practices. It is important for counselors trained in Western paradigms to consider how those paradigms can be adapted for counseling across cultures (Tanaka-Matsumi & Higginbotham, 1996). This includes acknowledgement of the limitations of counseling practices and consideration of incorporating indigenous healing methods that may be more acceptable to international students. One important area for review is the use of traditional assessment and testing instruments. Problems of cultural bias in standardized testing are well documented, along with recommendations for incorporating culture into formal and informal assessment methods (e.g., Dana, 1998; Paniagua, 2001). Assessment of international student concerns also requires skills for exploring how their problem would be viewed in their home culture, and how it would be managed. Incorporating a cultural assessment of client issues can provide valuable clues for designing an effective counseling intervention. Counselors may be able to incorporate indigenous therapies into their own repertoire of interventions, or build connections with local resource people who could assist in the facilitation of alternative counseling methods.

Spiritual dimensions of defining problems and the incorporation of spirituality has been undervalued in Western paradigms. Culturally skilled counselors must not only examine their own beliefs about religion and spirituality, but be prepared to consider these important dimensions in the lives of many clients from diverse cultures (Fukuyama & Sevig, 1999; McLennan, Rochow, & Arthur, 2001). Counselors also benefit from learning about models of helping that are holistic in nature, and that incorporate the spiritual dimension (e.g., Diller, 1999; Lecca, Quervalu, Nenes, & Gonzales, 1998). Counselors trained in Western paradigms of counseling typically emphasize the individual, and rely on verbal and emotional expression, self-disclosure, and client insight (Diller, 1999; Sue et al., 1998). It is important to appreciate that there are many ways to view reality and the client's self-concept and overt behaviors are only partial cues. Counselors can increase their skill competencies for assessment and interventions through reviewing models that consider other dimensions such as spirituality, events, conditions and experiences in the client's life (Axelson, 1999). Whatever choices a counselor makes in proceeding with counseling interventions needs to be centered in the potential benefits to clients. Counselors who work with international students require skills to assess client issues, and skills to design counseling interventions that make sense to students and that make a positive difference in their lives.

5.6   Multicultural   Counseling   Competencies: Organizational Development

The multicultural counseling competencies in the first three domains of self-awareness, knowledge, and skills are focused on the worldviews of counselors and clients and insuring that their professional practices are culturally responsive. However, counseling occurs in a context; counseling international students occurs in the context of a student service within a larger educational institution. The policies and procedures of a counseling office must also be examined for to consider potential barriers and ways to open access to diverse student populations. This point is most applicable to international students who are reported to underutilize counseling services (Anderson & Myer, 1985; Pedersen, 1991). The systems and organizations that surround counseling services must be carefully examined to consider ways that institutional culture may impede the success of clients who are culturally diverse (Sue et al., 1998). Organizational development is a key competency in educational institutions for responding to the needs of international students.

5.6.1   Internationalizing Counseling Services

Gaps exist between efforts to recruit higher numbers of international students and the responsiveness of institutions in providing adequate infrastructure (Arthur, 1997). These gaps raise serious questions about the ethics of recruiting students when services are not adequately in place to retain them. Institutions that do not infuse diversity into its structures and whose business and counseling practices are not relevant to international students will likely not be successful in international education. With increasing attention to internationalization, more attention has been paid to the contributions of international students and to ways that campus services need to be designed to support their needs (Dei, 1992; Diambomba, 1993; Francis, 1993). As most educational institutions now have a mandate pertaining to internationalization, counseling services must consider how they are contributing to internationalization. In turn, counselors are key resource people for internationalization through organizational development in other areas of campus.

5.6.1.1 Strategic Planning

Counseling services can begin with holding a strategic planning session with the explicit purpose of examining how well they serve culturally diverse students, including international students. In preparation for the session, counselors can read background information about specific student populations and consult with student leaders about issues pertaining to service delivery. Pragmatic issues such as hours of service, time allocated for counseling appointments, formats of delivering services, and outreach to other areas on campus are important agenda items. Support staff should be included in these discussions as they are often the first point of contact with an international student. When international students inquire about seeing a counselor, and scheduling does not permit immediate assistance, support staff need to be trained in going beyond a reply of "nobody is available to see you", to helping international students understand how services are offered and make every attempt to connect the student with a counselor. Resource material in counseling centers should be relevant for international students. Examples of materials include tip sheets for accessing campus resources, understanding and managing culture shock, and an introduction to counseling and the services offered to international students. Designing strategies for campus outreach is a critical part of strategic planning. A close liaison with the international student center on campus is essential for the purpose of collaboration in services and in opening the lines for student referral. Some post-secondary campuses have elected to decentralize their counseling staff to strengthen campus outreach efforts. A counselor whose office is located with the international student center is likely to achieve a higher profile with international students than when their office is in a separate area of campus.

5.6.1.2 Contributing to Campus Internationalization

Counselors can also contribute to internationalization through areas of campus outside of the counseling service office. For example, counselors could be part of an instructional team that designs and delivers workshops about internationalization, including the role of international students. Establishing venues for circulating information about international students can help to raise a positive profile of this student population. This also helps to dispel misconceptions about international students and improve the competencies of other staff members. In conjunction with the international student office and campus media services, information can be published in hard copy form such as newsletters or special bulletins designed for electronic circulation. The best way to help the campus move forward in being responsive to international students is to heighten their profile and to provide accurate information about their contributions and experiences. An institutional committee specifically designed to address the well being of international students provides focused and continual efforts to impact organizational development. Counselors have a pivotal role in negotiating the terms and direction of institutional efforts to host international students. Moving beyond an institutional mandate of internationalization to the implementation of practices that support international learners requires concerted efforts at both individual and organizational levels.

5.7 Bridging Domains of Multicultural Counseling Competencies

The material presented in this chapter was designed to introduce counselors to multicultural counseling competencies in the domains of self-awareness, knowledge, skills, and organizational development. Although this material was presented as four discrete domains, in reality, there is considerable overlap; learning and growth in one domain impacts other domains. Building multicultural counseling competencies requires a continuous process of reflection, knowledge acquisition, implementation of skills and services, and tracking progress through evaluation. The discussion has highlighted some implications of the competency domains for counseling international students, with suggestions for ways to improve counseling services, and ways to promote a responsive educational environment for international students.

6

Case Examples

6.   INTRODUCTION TO CASE EXAMPLES

Counsellors who work with international students are exposed to many issues associated with cross-cultural transition and adjustment to life in the host culture. It is fascinating to consider how a lens of culture helps to explain the experiences of international students. The variety of countries and cultures in an international student population means that similar transition issues are experienced in different ways. Counsellors need to remember that culture is an ever-present force in the transition demands that students face. Culture also influences how counsellors perceive student situations and the interventions that they offer. Multicultural counselling with international students requires counselors to be aware of their own perspectives about student issues, and be willing to learn about the specific meanings that students apply to their experiences. This opens the door for mutual learning about ways that transition issues can be addressed.

The following case examples are presented to illustrate some of the common issues and unique situations faced by international students. These are actual counselling cases, with the names of students changed to protect their identity. The case examples are written to help counsellors make connections between transition demands described in the literature, and how students actually experienced them. When reviewing the case examples, counsellors are encouraged to identify the core issues presented in each case, the confounding influences of culture, how the issue is addressed by the counsellor, and possible directions for counselling interventions. There is more than one way to define client issues and many options for counselling interventions. Each of these case examples could be approached with ideas about individual counselling, group counselling approaches such as orientation workshops and support groups, advocacy on behalf of students, and interventions to change the educational environment. It is hoped that counsellors find these examples useful to consider the following questions:
- What are the presenting client issues in this case?
- What cultural values are influencing the client's perception of the issues?

- What personal values of the counsellor might come into play in defining client issues or appropriate interventions?
- What interventions would help students to build their coping resources?
- What interventions to impact organizational change would help to support international students in the future?

These reflection questions are useful guides for reviewing the case studies presented in this chapter. They are also useful reflection questions for future counselling practice with international students.

6.1 Ramon: Miles away from Family

Ramon was a 32-year old student from Nigeria. His education was sponsored by a special scholarship by his government, in partnership with a development agency. Ramon made contact with counselling services after 2 months in his academic program. He began the conversation by sharing his initial excitement about coming to Canada. He noted that his parents were very proud of him, and his extended family honored him with a celebration before he left home. When I inquired about how his academic program was going, he replied, "School is very expensive and I want to do well for my family." This reply helped me to introduce some of the pressures that Ramon was feeling about academic success. He noted that the instructors were very good and that they were always willing to answer his questions. However, his relationships with student peers were less positive. He described trying to talk to the other students, but many of them did not seem very serious about their studies. He added, that most of the conversations with other students were one-sided.

> They ask me where I am from. When I tell them I am from Africa, they seem interested at first. I mention my home country, Nigeria, and they don't seem very interested. They typically ask me if it is hot there or if there is a lot of crime. I want to talk about more than the weather. I would like to talk about more important things like politics, about how our companies work in this area (of technology), but they show little interest. Most times, they change the subject and continue talking about things in Canada. I am very interested to learn about life in Canada, please do not misunderstand me. However, there are many things that I would share about life back home. Nobody here seems to care.

When I asked Ramon to elaborate about his relationships with instructors at the school, he hesitated, saying that he did not think it was appropriate to talk about them. I reassured Ramon about the confidentiality in discussing matters in counselling and that I would never speak to his instructors about his situation without his permission. After a long pause, he said that he found it interesting how instructors presented their material and he liked the practical examples that they offered. After another long pause in the conversation, he added, "there are other ways to do things that what teachers here say. I have worked for many years and would like to offer my experience. But I am a student here and they are the teachers." I asked Ramon if there were any specific instructors that he felt he could approach about his professional experience. After thinking about his for a minute, he said, "Jim, the instructor for operations management, often makes a point of asking me how I am and how the course is going. He has offered to meet with me if I have any questions. Maybe he thinks that I don't understand the material."

Ramon and I continued to talk about each of his classes and which instructors he thought were more approachable. I explained that offers to provide students with extra assistance were meant as a gesture of support and, if anything, it meant that the teacher was interested in making sure that students had a positive learning experience. Ramon agreed that he would follow-up with his instructor, Jim, this week, to try to engage him in a discussion about application of the course material to his work situation at home.

Before closing the session, I revisited Ramon's comment that school was very expensive, noting the high price of tuition for international students and that many students find the cost of living in Canada to be higher than they expected. Ramon replied in a quiet voice, "It is hard for me to talk about these matters. It makes me feel weak. I cannot ask my family to give more than they have to help me come to school." After gently encouraging Ramon to discuss his finances, he disclosed that he was having difficulty finding enough money to buy food and new clothes needed for the winter months. We discussed some practical suggestions about places to shop in the city with inexpensive prices on personal items like food and clothes. I also asked Ramon if he would be interested in part-time employment. Due to immigration restrictions, he would have to be employed on campus. His expression brightened at the suggestion, and he said, "I am not afraid of work; I will be glad for anything you can give me." I referred Ramon to a colleague in the student employment center to discuss part-time jobs on campus and the methods of applying for those jobs. With Ramon's permission, I contacted the colleague, to let him know that I made the referral, asking him to consider the immediacy of Ramon's need for employment. This networking helped Ramon to gain employment for a 2-month contract. The academic department that hired him was very satisfied with his work and found another project for him to continue for the remainder of the academic year.

Once Ramon's concrete needs were met for financial assistance, and for presenting his professional expertise with personnel in his academic program, he was much happier about his experience as an international student. I followed up with one more formal counselling appointment with this student, primarily as a measure to make sure he followed up with his course instructor, to make sure his employment was going well, and to demonstrate a genuine interest in his well-being. I met Ramon several times on campus that year and always made a point of stopping to chat informally with him.

Midway through the academic year, Ramon came to the counselling center without an appointment. The receptionist came to see me and said that Ramon looked very distressed, and would not meet with the counsellor who was available for drop-in clients that day. When I met with Ramon, he was devastated after receiving a letter from his mother with news that one of his uncles had passed away in Nigeria. He was full of grief and concern for his family. Ramon talked about the difficulties of being in Canada when he wanted to be home with his family. I asked him to describe what he would do if he were at home. He described that as the oldest son, he would have responsibilities to represent the family and that the family would gather for a celebration to commemorate the life of this uncle. Ramon was very upset that he could not take care of his family in this way and spoke of how cut off he felt from his family. As an immediate intervention, I offered that Ramon could call his parents from the privacy of my office. This sense of urgency to connect with his family seemed paramount. As this student did not have resources to fly home for the funeral, we discussed ways that he could make a contribution. He decided to write letters to his aunt and to his father, outlining special memories of his uncle and to let them know how much he cared about his uncle. I continued to meet with Ramon for two more sessions, to provide grief counselling. I explained a model of grief that was used by professional counsellors and asked Ramon to describe how grief was experienced in his country. This interchange of cultural perspectives was informative, and it opened the discussion for Ramon to talk about his personal feelings of distance from his family at such an important time.

The last contact that I had with Ramon was when he dropped into the counselling office to tell me that he had received a job in his professional field, for 1 year following the completion of his academic program. He was thrilled to have this opportunity, noting that this employment experience would be highly valued when he returned home the following year.

6.2 Mindy: Love between Cultures

Mindy was a 24-year-old student from China who was enrolled in a business degree program. She initiated an appointment with me to review her study skills techniques for managing her academic program. Mindy presented as an extremely bright and articulate woman who was clear about her professional goals. She chose to study in Canada initially for her undergraduate program, but her ultimate dream was to continue on to a graduate program in a prestigious university such as Harvard. She was very motivated in her academic program and wanted to make sure that she was doing everything that she could to succeed. This session was not problem-focused. It was centered on prevention of academic issues through a review of Mindy's study habits and strategies. Mostly, she seemed to need reassurance that she was "on track" and doing everything that she could to be academically successful.

My contact with Mindy continued on an informal basis as she participated in social functions planned for international students. She offered to make a presentation about her home city as part of an internationalization initiative for staff and students on campus to learn about different cultures. She made considerable efforts to prepare her material and the presentation was well received by the audience. At the end of the presentation, a man came to meet her and it was obvious that they were very attracted to each other. Mindy made a point of introducing me to her friend. She said that she would make an appointment with me to discuss my opinion of her presentation.

The following week, Mindy came for an appointment but it was soon obvious that the agenda would not be concerning her presentation. She seemed very anxious, and began crying as she spoke. She apologized profusely for crying, saying that she was very embarrassed about needing to speak to me about private matters, however, she said that she felt she had nobody else that she could confide in. I tried to reassure Mindy that if she was upset, that it was all right to shed tears. She did not receive this reassurance, and it only seemed to heighten her embarrassment about presenting in a way that was out of control. I asked Mindy if something had happened to prompt her sense of anxiety. She replied that she thought she might be in trouble and needed help to decide what to do. Mindy disclosed that she was married to a man in her home country, but came to Canada when she learned that her husband was unfaithful to her. At first, her husband agreed to the situation and provided financial resources for her. He had been to visit her once in Canada, and seemed very displeased with her. Communication with her had been cut off, however, she had recently learned from a friend that he had asked people in Canada to "check up" on her. I admitted to Mindy that I was confused about the meaning of these events, but I asked her directly if she thought she might be harmed. She replied, "My husband is a powerful man with lots of money. That is why I married him. I am his first wife and that should mean something. If he is not happy with me, then I am uncertain what he might do." During this disclosure, Mindy scrutinized my reactions very carefully. I immediately commented about the significance of her status as "first wife". Mindy proudly commented that her husband asked to meet her after she competed in a beauty contest for a title highly prized in her culture. Mindy added that she knew her husband would be with other women, however, when he stopped spending any time with her, she decided to pursue her own career. We reviewed a plan for safety, including whom she could trust at home and in the local culture, and where she would go to live if she felt unsafe in her apartment. Mindy also agreed to let me know if anything changed and that she would call me office and leave a message during the next 3 weeks letting me know she was all right.

I felt compelled to bring up with Mindy what I had observed between she and her friend at the multicultural presentation. I made it clear that she only had to talk about him if she wanted. Mindy laughed and said, "You can see that I am in love with him." From there, we discussed some of the choices that Mindy thought she was facing in her future. She raised concerns about losing status in her home country if she was to pursue a divorce but admitted that she was hoping that her husband would initiate these proceedings. Her relationship with her friend in Canada was making her happy, however, she was concerned that her husband would find out. We discussed the double standard that operated in her culture, and how it would be seen differently for her to take a lover outside of the marriage in comparison to her husband. Mindy also discussed her reservations about getting too involved with a Canadian man. She said that her career plans were her primary concern and that her relationships would come second. Throughout this session, I reflected back the values that Mindy seemed to be expressing, and the potential conflicts that she was describing between achievement and relationships. When she inquired about relationships in Canada, I told her that I was most willing to discuss my experience and perceptions, but that was not representative of all women in Canada. This openness to talk about gender issues, values about marriage and fidelity, and choice points about career and relationships helped Mindy to feel calmer about her issues. I also made a point of complimenting Mindy for her strengths and wisdom to make choices for herself. Her sense of determination was clearly an asset that would see her through difficult decisions. Mindy kept in contact through phone to let me know she was okay. At the end of the academic year, she wrote me a thank you note and let me know that she was pursuing graduate studies in her academic field.

6.3   Mikael: Honesty in Academic Work

Mikael was a student from Russia who travelled with ten other students from Russia. The group was enrolled in the same academic program and attended classes together, along with local students. I met Mikael at an orientation for the students from Russia. His verbal English skills were noticeably stronger than his peers, and he seemed more confident about interacting with people in the host culture. In consultation with the international student advisor, we asked Mikael to be the contact person for the group for any programming needs and to meet with the international student advisor if the group had any concerns. He accepted this responsibility willingly. Later in the year, as part of an international student services publication, several students from different countries were asked to contribute their perspectives in writing about their experiences as an international student. After Mikael made his submission, one of the international student advisors came to see me as she recognized the material that Mikael contributed from another source. It had been plagiarized and was about to be published as if original work. We agreed that it would be more appropriate for the international student advisor who knew Mikael and who recognized the problem with the material to meet with him. She explained the implications of publishing material that had been written by someone else, including the potential consequences of plagiarism for Mikael, and the embarrassment it could cause in a publication from the student services office.

About 2 months later, the Dean of the academic program that Mikael was enrolled in called me to discuss a matter involving cheating on an exam. Mikael was reprimanded for speaking to his peers during written exam. As the language used in the exchange was Russian, the instructor could not be certain if he was cheating. However, the instructor was concerned, as during a previous exam, there was a problem with Mikael looking over at another student's work. I agreed to see Mikael if he was willing to come and talk to me.

When Mikael arrived at my office, he came with the assumption that I wanted to talk to him about how the group from Russia was faring, and he was not aware that his instructor had referred him to discuss the accusations of cheating. This was immediately a source of embarrassment for him. I was concerned about whether Mikael would stay in the office and, out of fear of reprimand, decide to leave. To approach the topic, I began saying the things that I had noticed about Mikael at the student orientation. I also told him that he struck me as somebody mature enough to be able to talk about difficult issues. I made it very clear that my job was not to reprimand him or give information back to his instructors. My purpose was to talk to him about academic honesty and to keep him from getting into further difficulties. At that point, I gave Mikael the choice to stay or to leave my office. He decided to stay and said that he was willing to talk about the situation.

I approached this delicate matter by saying that I did not understand why Mikael might have difficulties completing his academic work. I added that he had always struck me as a person with considerable integrity, and this did not fit my image of him. Mikael thanked me for the compliments and then asked if he could be frank with me, which I encouraged. He commented, "People here make a big deal about these things. At home, it is not a big deal. Everybody helps everybody else. If one of my friends asks me for an answer on an exam, I give it to him. It is expected. We help each other out. That is the way it is done." I then asked Mikael about the situation when an instructor thought she saw him looking at another student's work. Mikael said he had learned from that situation. "After the exam, the student, a woman, came up to me and told me not to do that again. She said almost the same things that you did, that I did not need to cheat, that I could do this on my own." This gave us an opportunity to discuss how his behavior was viewed by peers from his home culture in comparison to how his behavior might be seen by other students and instructors in the host culture. Mikael agreed there were differences and that he would have to think about what he wanted.

During our session, I introduced the campus policy about academic integrity in work and the consequences of plagiarism. It was important to make sure that Mikael understood the severity of the matter from the point of view of campus policy. I assured Mikael that I would not disclose our conversation with anyone else, that it was important for me to meet with him to go over these matters, and that he was free to contact me in the future if he wished to discuss anything else. This was a difficult interview with this student, as there were fine lines between supporting him, and acting as an authority for the educational institution. However, it was important to let him know about how his behavior would be seen in the local cultural context, and to help him explore options about maintaining his friendships with peers without jeopardizing his academic program.

6.4   Hiroshi: Whose Life Is It?

Hiroshi was a 20-year-old student from Japan who made an appointment to see me to talk about difficulties he was having in his academic program. Hiroshi was enrolled in the second year of a business degree program. His grades were marginally passing and he was concerned about the upcoming final exams. I began by asking Hiroshi about each of his courses and what he liked and did not like about them. His affect was stilted and he did not give me eye contact during this conversation. His general demeanor prompted me to wonder if he was depressed, but I did not have sufficient information to draw anything but tentative conclusions. In response to questions about his health, he admitted that he was having problems falling asleep at night, he felt constantly tired, and he had minimal appetite. He was difficult to engage in a conversation about his academic program or his study skills so I decided to change the topic of conversation and later come back to these issues.

When I asked Hiroshi what he enjoyed in his time away from school, there was a remarkable change in his manner of presentation. He described his love of drawing and how he would spend hours sketching scenes from his home and areas of Calgary that he liked to visit. He offered to show me his sketch book. His voice was filled with enthusiasm as he described his drawings. As we were finishing looking at the sketches, I asked the question, "Hiroshi, why are you pursuing a business program that you are so unhappy in, when your real passion seems to be art?" Hiroshi changed back to his first manner of presentation and quietly said, "My father wants me to take business, he does not think that art is worthwhile." My immediate reaction to this disclosure was to want to encourage Hiroshi to pursue what he wanted to, and that the decision about his career choice was his own to make. Holding back on this reaction was difficult for me as I could see the stress that this student was experiencing. He described feeling little motivation to study courses such as accounting and marketing that held little interest. The only thing that seemed to motivate him was the dreaded alternative of failing his program and facing his father. I explained to Hiroshi that I could help him to explore other career options if that is what he wanted, or we could work on helping him feel better about his choice to stay in the business program. This opened up the conversation, as he had not previously considered that he had choices. I carefully made a point of emphasizing with him that I was not suggesting that he discontinue studies in the business program. Rather, I thought that he had choices within the program, or to look at other options, each would have benefits and consequences. We explored what he perceived as the consequences of leaving the business program and he stated that he felt the costs to him personally and to his family at this time were too great.

In the next appointment, Hiroshi gladly told me that he had passed all of his exams. However, his manner of presentation continued to suggest depression, and I again inquired about symptoms and signs of depression. I asked Hiroshi if there was anything else going on in his life that was causing him to feel so stressed. Hiroshi quietly told me that he thought he was a homosexual, and that he felt anguish about this realization. He said he had to tell somebody about his feelings but was full of shame for he knew his family would reject him if they found out he had feelings for other men. Hiroshi described how he had limited attraction to women and that he found men easier to be around. Since his time in the host country, he felt that it was freer for him to explore this attraction to men, as the local culture seemed more accepting of homosexuality. I cautioned Hiroshi that this might be true in general terms, but it would still be important for him to be selective about who he came out to in Canadian society. We discussed ways that he might connect with other students about their experiences, and I provided him with information about associations on campus and resources in the gay community.

During the next 5 sessions of working together, Hiroshi and I talked about a recurring theme, how he was leading a life to please his family at home, and how he experienced life in Canada. Many issues, including his vocational choice, future career choice, and his sexual identity seemed to have parallel themes, according to whether he wanted to follow family tradition and values, or whether he wanted to explore new ways of living. At first, Hiroshi seemed to be rejecting a lot of his home culture in preference for more liberal ways of thinking in Canada. Simultaneously, the strong emotions that Hiroshi was experiencing led me to believe that he still held strong allegiance to his home culture. I encouraged him to tell me about the aspects of his home culture that he missed and parts of his culture that he thought were strengths. In a parallel fashion, I tried to help Hiroshi see that his choices were not "all or nothing" in which his only options were allegiance to his family and personal misery, or following his personal preferences and losing his family. At this time, he felt that it was important for him to explore his sexuality and to come to terms with his attraction to other men. We discussed the experiences of other gay men in keeping this information away from family and how to decide about coming out to other people. In the meantime, Hiroshi made the decision that he should finish his business program. In his own words, he said, "That is something that I can do for my father." As part of career planning, we looked at settings where he could be in the art world, and still maintain the legitimacy of a career using his business degree. We also discussed ways for Hiroshi to connect with other artists and to pursue his love of drawing. Explaining to him that notions of career in North America extended past one's work role helped Hiroshi reframe that what he chose to do in his time away from work could still be valued.

6.5   Ronnie: Home Is Where My Heart Lies

Ronnie was a female student from Japan, who was I met through a reception at the beginning of the year for international students. She set up an appointment to see me as she remembered during a brief presentation at the reception that I worked with students who had academic problems. Ronnie said that her parents had encouraged her to pursue a foreign education, and laughed as she said, "they almost drove the plane here so that I would leave home." Ronnie said that she initially felt very excited about coming to Canada but now was not so sure if it was a good idea. She admitted missing her family and crying herself to sleep most nights. She said that she found it very difficult to make friends at school as students seemed too busy to talk. Even though she was living in residence where there were lots of people around, she said that she felt very lonely living there. Studying in her second language was more difficult than she expected and so she spent most nights in her room going over class material and reading. I asked Ronnie if she would like to try an exercise where she could repack her suitcase with anything that she missed from home. She lit up with this idea and mentioned several types of food, things from her room at home, and then she laughed and asked if was allowed to pack a few people in her suitcase. If was obvious that this student was extremely homesick. I was concerned about the degree of stress that she was experiencing, her lack of connection with people in the host culture, and concerns that she had about her academic program.

When I inquired about her academic program, Ronnie said that her courses were interesting, however, she was having problems. This did not seem to be related to academic ability as her recent grades were well above a passing mark. Rather, her concerns centered on the interpersonal behavior of teachers and students.

> *Classes here are so different than the way that I was taught at home. Here, everybody talks at once. The teachers don't always teach; they seem to let the students run the class. I want to learn more from the teachers. The students can be very rude. They interrupt the teachers and each other; we would never do that at home. It is hard to know how to prepare for classes. We are supposed to do all of this reading on our own, but sometimes we don't even talk about the material assigned to the course. It takes me a long time to go through the readings, but they are all important. The other day, we were supposed to be working on our group project. I like to wait to hear what the other students have to say, and then make my contribution. However, they made all of the decisions about how we would do the*

assignment, and did not ask my opinion. They just told me what was my part. It does not feel like they even want me in the group.

Ronnie and I talked about the differences in instructor-student relationships between her home country and some of the local teaching and learning practices. I encouraged her to participate in activities organized for international students so that she could connect with other students, and perhaps share some of her experiences. She was initially very reluctant about agreeing to this suggestion, saying that she did not have time to do anything else. I reiterated the importance of building social connections in the local culture and she agreed to try one activity.

About 3 months later, a male international student dropped by the office to see me. Chi-Ping told me that he came to see me about his girlfriend, Ronnie, as he knew that Ronnie had met with me during the previous semester. I immediately told Chi-Ping that I could not discuss the content of my meeting with Ronnie, but I would listen to what he had to say. Chi-Ping told me that he was worried about Ronnie and that he did not know what to do. He described that she was having health problems, had developed a major rash on her face and body. She was beginning to miss classes and seemed to lose interest in a lot of things. She had told Chi-Ping that she had recently thought about committing suicide. I asked Chi-Ping's permission to call Ronnie and tell her that he had come to see me. Ethically, I was obligated to try to make contact with Ronnie, given the possibility of suicide ideation. I telephoned Ronnie and asked if she would come and talk to me. She said that she did not really want to but would come because I asked her to.

In the second appointment with this student, I noticed a major deterioration in her health. Her face was covered in a rash that looked like eczema, she had lost weight since our last appointment, and there was little change in affect as she spoke. I noted the concern that Chi-Ping had expressed and that I, too, was concerned about how she was faring as a student in Canada. After a period of silence, she looked at me, and said, "I just don't think I can do this anymore." I immediately clarified my understanding of what she meant by this statement, in case she meant taking her life. Ronnie said that she had tried her best to succeed as an international student, but it just was not working. Ironically, this student was excelling in her academic program. However, her feelings about "not fitting in" were overpowering any sense of personal efficacy. When I asked Ronnie what she wanted to do, she adamantly stated, "I just want to go home." We discussed what that would mean for her and her family if she decided to go home. Ronnie was relieved to learn that she could take a semester off from her academic program and return if that was her choice. After exploring her situation, she decided that she would tell her parents about her unhappiness and ask them if she could return home. The next day, Ronnie came back to see me and was obviously relieved. During her conversation with her parents, they agreed that she should come home and they would support her to make a decision about her school program. Ronnie felt that she could "tough it out" for the remaining month of the semester. I included a suicide risk assessment in this interview as well as a referral to medical services for physiological symptoms of culture shock. We scheduled one more appointment to follow upon on some presenting health concerns, and Ronnie agreed to contact me more often if she had any further thoughts about suicide.

Six months later, Ronnie came to see me again for a brief appointment. She had spent the previous semester in Japan with her family, and was able to work at a job related to her academic program. She told me that the time at home was just what she had needed. It gave her a chance to re-evaluate her plans to be an international student and she now felt more ready to face being so far away from home. She also commented about her observations of culture. "When I was here, all that I could think about was my life at home. I expected that everything would be perfect when I returned to my family. It was nice, but I remembered things about living there that were not so easy. I found myself missing parts of life here and that really surprised me. I guess that I am lucky to have the choice. My parents were really good about the decision. Last time I felt pushed about coming here; this time it was my choice. And I remembered what you said about the suitcase, that I can bring what I want from my culture with me." Ronnie was fortunate in that she had resources to return to her home country, as she needed. Many other international students are away from their family and friends for the entire duration of their time as an international student. In this case, travel home helped Ronnie gain perspective about her life from two cultural points of view.

6.6   Mannie: Defining Masculinity

Mannie was a 24-year old student from Malaysia. When he first arrived in the host culture, he spent a lot of time in the international student office, coming in every day to say hi to the staff and tell them something about his day. He quickly became well known by the staff and everyone liked him. He openly expressed his appreciation to staff for their kindness and eagerly participated in social activities offered for international students. Over several months, the staff noticed considerable changes in Mannie's behavior. Whereas he used to dress in clothes from his homeland, his style of dress changed to Western fashion. One of the staff joked with him that they had never seen so many designer labels on a person at one time. Mannie joked back with the staff, commenting that he really liked trying out new things in the host culture, as so many things were better than life at home. As another month passed, Mannie's mannerisms began to change. The formerly jovial student seemed to change into a student who was not very happy. The staff commented to me that they were concerned about Mannie and how he was adjusting to life in Canada.

Mannie was an active participant in a support group for international students. The group was organized to provide a weekly time for international students to come together and talk about issues of concern and for problem-solving. As the group facilitator, I quickly learned that an open-ended agenda was not very effective. Students were not sure what to talk about or what was the purpose of the group. One of the students asked if we could set a topic for each week to talk about life in Canadian culture. This was enthusiastically received by other students and seemed to be a viable way to add enough structure to increase comfort for participation. We identified several topics of interest to the students and I suggested some topics that would help students learn about how issues might be viewed from various cultures. Structure at the beginning of the group helped students to engage in conversation, and the discussion could flow in areas of interest to them.

Mannie attended most of the groups and I, too, observed the changes mentioned by other staff in the international student office. After one of the groups finished, Mannie asked if he could stay and talk to me. He opened up the conversation by saying that he did not like life in Canada and that he was disappointed in many of the people that he had met. I expressed my surprise at this statement, given how complimentary he had been previously about his preference for the clothing and ways of living in this culture. Mannie explained that he realized that much of what he liked was "on the surface" but with more time here, he had discovered that there were a lot of contradictions about Canadian values and lifestyles. He mentioned that he found it especially confusing in trying to make friendships. I asked him to give me some examples of situations that had bothered him.

> *Well, it is like this. People here say, "Hi, how are you?" and then they walk away. I just get ready to tell them and then they are gone. I am never sure if people mean what they commit to. I thought that I had made a new friend in class. Melinda asked me to her house for a party and I went and had a really good time. She said that we should go for lunch. I waited outside her class 3 days in a row. On the third day, she came by but she told me she was too busy to go for lunch. What seems like a yes turns out to be a no.*

Mannie and I talked about his confusion, and how he was learning about some of the nuances of social interactions in the local culture. I challenged him about what I was hearing in terms of judgments about culture. It seemed that Mannie was struggling, in part, through a comparison of his home culture and the new culture, in which one culture had to "win" and be better than the other. I then explored with him some specific aspects of life in Canada since he arrived and how well he thought he was managing. After several minutes, Mannie stated that he realized how far he had come since his arrival in Canada, however, in other ways, it felt like he was still at the beginning. He agreed to make a journal about his experience and come and see me in 2 weeks.

Another situation arose with this student that posed a challenge for counselling. Another international student from the support group came to speak to me and said that she was not going to come back to the group. She explained that one of the other group members made her feel uncomfortable and she did not want to deal with him. She offered several examples where Mannie had approached her. At first she liked him because he was polite and considerate. Recently, she noticed that he was very aggressive and she was beginning to become afraid of him. This scenario happened at the same time as I had noticed a change in Mannie's behavior with other staff in the international student office. Whereas Mannie used to have impeccable manners, his style of presenting seemed more abrupt and, especially with the female staff, he seemed to be overly flirtatious. One of the staff members commented that "it was too bad, he used to be such a nice guy."

When Mannie came back to see me, I decided that one of the things that might be important to discuss with him was his view of gender roles across cultures. I began by asking him how he observed male and female students interacting together, and what he had learned. He explained that there were a lot of differences between how men acted in public in his home country, in comparison to what he saw in Canada. He said that he was initially shocked at the openness through which men approached women in Canada. However, he said that he was trying to be more like men here. I chose to share with Mannie some of my concerns about how he might be received by women with his current style of interacting. He was initially embarrassed and asked if he had offended me somehow. I assured him that it was because I thought he was such a good person that I wanted to have this discussion with him, and that it might be important for him to consider how other women might perceive his behavior. I also chose to share with Mannie some of the comments that I had heard from staff and students about qualities that they admired and liked about him. At the end of the discussion, I concluded by saying that it seemed that others liked him most when he was himself, and not trying to act like somebody else. Mannie smiled at this suggestion and told me that he felt a sense of relief. He added that it was confusing to know where he stood in relationships in the host culture, but he was very sure where he stood with me. He revisited some of the confusion that he had felt about how to fit in with social relations and that he was especially concerned that women might not accept him. As a course of action, we agreed up on a goal of taking pressure off from trying to date women, and to work on developing friendships first. Mannie said that was consistent with how many of his best relationships had developed at home.

A key aspect of our work together over five sessions of counselling was helping Mannie to reconcile areas of his personal identity. We used a validationgram (Ishiyama, 1995b) as a tool to help explore notions of self in life roles since becoming an international student, including his academic self, family relationships, leisure, and I deliberately added the category of male role expectations as an area to be explored. This tool helped Mannie to continue his comparison of norms and values between his home and host culture and he was able to identify areas from both cultures that he found to be desirable. As a symbol of his cultural journey, I noticed during his last appointment with me that he wore a shirt that was not of Western style. When I commented about the design and colours of his shirt, he proudly announced, "This one is from home, and I decided it was time to start wearing it again."

6.7   Jenine: Breaking Away From Gender Roles

Jenine was a 22-year-old student from Eastern Europe who was coming to the end of her academic program. She attended a re-entry workshop that I facilitated for students who were going to be finishing their academic program and returning home in the next month. The group members attending the workshop were from the same country and that allowed us to focus on some specific cultural issues. The group proceeded through a review of aspects of culture that they enjoyed in Canada and what they thought they would miss. Jenine was a very vocal participant in the group. She initiated a discussion about her concern for losing her language proficiency in English when she returned home. Other group members shared similar concerns about working hard to overcome language barriers, and they were afraid that their competencies would soon deteriorate without daily practice. As the workshop progressed, Jenine became obviously distressed. When the topic of discussion came to looking ahead to life at home, Jenine said that she did not want to look ahead, she just wanted to party while she could. She wanted to make the most of the last few weeks in the host country because she knew that her life would never be the same. As the workshop progressed, she became very quiet and did not contribute to the discussion. At the end of the workshop, I made a point of saying goodbye to Jenine and thanked her for her important contributions to the discussion. I added that if there was anything that she wanted to talk about with respect to returning home, that I would be glad to meet with her in my office where other students would not be around. Jenine said that she would think about it and quickly left the workshop.

Later that week, she followed up by making an appointment to see me. When I asked what she would like to talk to me about, she said that the workshop was very upsetting for her. Jenine said that before the workshop, she was enjoying her life in Canada, and even though she knew she would eventually have to go home, she was just focusing on the weeks that she could enjoy herself. When I probed about what came up for her in the workshop, she replied,

> I was really angry with you that day. It was like you burst a bubble around me. I had not thought much about life at home. Then a lot of things came rushing back. I had not thought about personal safety for a long time and then thought of not being able to walk freely on the streets. I began to think about what it will be like to go home and live with my family. I love my family, but I have changed since moving here. I have lived on my own for the first time in my life. When I go back, I will be my father's daughter again and he will have to o.k. every move that I make. That will be very difficult. And I began to realize that school will be over, and maybe this is the last chance for me to get an education. I have loved being a student here. We have learned so many new things, not just in class, but about life. There is a lot of freedom here. I don't want to leave school; I want to keep learning. I don't know if there will be other opportunities for me at home.

In responding to Jenine, I tried very hard to validate her feelings and used several feeling words to try to capture what she was experiencing. She picked up on the words scared and angry and said that it was hard for her to be experiencing these feelings and concentrate on her school program during the final weeks. She stated that she did not want this to take over the many positive experiences that she had as an international student, but the recent negative feelings were overpowering.

I asked Jenine if she would be willing to explore each of the areas of concern that she had mentioned and asked her to choose a starting point. In reviewing each area, I asked her to think about what she had gained through living and learning as an international student, and what she felt that might be lost when she returned home. I also encouraged her to think about ways that she might be able to incorporate her new learning into various roles at home. One of the concrete decisions that appeared helpful to her was information about how to access university programs in countries close to her home and how to check out admission requirements and the transferability of some of her university credits. We also brainstormed ways for her to continue practicing her English language skills that were so closely connected to her sense of identity as an international student. Jenine was very excited about the possibility of teaching English to students in her home country. She exclaimed, "I could do this in the evening as a way to get out of the house!"

I invited Jenine to talk about her fears of returning home and the restrictions that she would experience as a woman in her culture. This was a difficult discussion for both of us. Jenine was most upset about this aspect of her re-entry transition, and described it as "going home to suffocate." I shared with her my concern over the restrictions in her life, but did not want to impose my values about the roles between men and women in her country. At best, I was able to muster a question about the potential benefits and traditions in those roles. Jenine seemed to lighten in her discussion about some of the advantages that she saw in comparison to examples of lifestyles of women in the host culture. At the end, she stated, "What bothers me most is that I feel like my choices will be taken away from me." Jenine added that she was seriously considering not returning home but was stalled in her efforts to obtain a change in her immigration status. This added another level of seriousness to the discussion as I asked Jenine to describe the implications this would have for her relationships with her family. She responded that she knew she her family would disown her, mostly her father, but the rest of the family would have to follow his decision.

In the counselling role, I was very concerned about how this student's decision-making about not returning home might impact her family relationships. I was concerned that a choice she made now could ultimately determine the course of family relations for the rest of her life. To explore this further, I asked her to think about what her life might be like without any contact with her family, now, in 5 years, when she decided to get married, and when she had children. Although it was difficult for her to project that far in the future, she was able to connect with the potential difficulties of no contact with her family if she became a mother. "I cannot imagine what it would be like for me not be able to introduce my children to the rest of the family, or have them help with their care. What would I tell them?" I framed Jenine's portrayal of her situation as a dilemma about not being able to live with her family, and not being able to live without them. She said that she realized that she could not live without them, but had been avoiding thinking about how she could return home and live with them. We explored her sources of social support within the family, other women in the family who might be sympathetic towards restrictions on female gender roles, and how she could keep in touch with the friends that she had made as an international student. As we finished the session, Jenine stated that she had come to realize that her time as an international student might be the best time in her life. She added that she was very sad that it was coming to an end, but that she was determined to find ways to keep learning and to pursue her education.

The re-entry process for this student would undoubtedly be difficult. Jenine experienced the abruptness of finishing life in the host culture and returning home. Although her experience in the re-entry workshop had prompted a strong emotional reaction, this helped her move into a place where she could begin to anticipate her life at home. Rather than defining her life as "over', she began to consider options for herself that would continue her path of learning. Her anticipation of returning to traditional gender roles is a common theme for women international students who find new freedoms in the host culture. However, it is very important for counsellors to be cautious about judging the ways that gender roles are organized in various cultures. Many women continue to appreciate positive aspects of their culture and may feel even more conflicted if the counsellor seemingly judges their home culture. For some international students, re-entry issues are inextricably tied to ways of reconciling their new learning about culture with norms about gender and life roles at home.

7

Enhancing Counseling Services for International Students

7. EXPANDING THE SCOPE OF COUNSELING SERVICES

Designing counseling services requires counselors to consider the emerging needs of international students at various stages of cross-cultural transition. Students have specific needs during the transition of entering the new culture as they begin their academic program and face new situations and new ways of interacting. As international students master early demands and learn about the local culture, their counseling issues also change in focus. Likewise, as students begin to prepare for leaving the host country and returning home, the nature of the issues that are relevant for counseling are often related to re-entry. Counseling services need to take into consideration the shifting concerns of international students and consider how their services can be organized to be responsive. This requires counselors to move "beyond narrowly defined methods and contexts" (Pedersen, 1991, p. 29) and take a dynamic approach to the design and delivery of counseling services.

7.1 Directions for Counseling Services

There are four dimensions or avenues that have been identified to systematically organize counseling services for international students (Hammer, 1992). First, services need to adopt a "problems focus" which addresses the pragmatic needs of students that are often heightened during the initial stage of cross-cultural transition, i.e., housing, course selection, employment and financial matters. Second, a "counseling focus" requires international students to have access to culturally competent counselors and advisors who are willing to work with students in a variety of formats including individual counseling, psychoeducational workshops, and support groups. Third, "interaction and communication focus" supports international students to connect with other students through co-national, bicultural, and multicultural networks on campus. Peer training and the involvement of other international students are important programming components. Services in this avenue should also consider support for local students who are interested in pursuing meaningful relationships with international students. Local students may need training to help them appreciate the influence of culture on interpersonal relationships and to help them appreciate the interpersonal issues faced by international students (Arthur, 1997). This also enhances the probability that cultural learning in bi-cultural relationships will be reciprocated. Fourth, a "culture learning focus" involves services that support internationalizing the local context, including lectures, discussions, and tours (Hammer, 1992). Again, an essential feature of services is to encourage reciprocal learning between international students and the individuals they interact with on campus and in the local community.

7.1.1   Expanding Counselor Roles

Counselors have a pivotal role to play in the design and delivery of services in each of these four avenues. Undoubtedly, the majority of their time and their central role involve the "counseling focus". However, to limit services to that role ignores the expertise that counselors can bring to a co-ordinated and systematic approach to service design and delivery (Sandu, 1994). As outlined in Chapter 5, counselors can serve as consultants to other student services and academic personnel about ways to increase the responsiveness to international students' needs. Counselors can also gain valuable understanding about international students through participating and offering their services in domains that have traditionally been considered outside of the "counseling focus." In turn, it is through contact with counselors, or during service delivery in the other three domains, that international students decide to pursue counseling offered through individual or group programming. The profile that counselors hold in campus internationalization supports referral of international students to counseling services. Both academic and support staff need to be informed about the ways that counselors can assist international students. One of the most important goals of any counseling intervention with international students is to help them strengthen their network of social support (Chen, 1999; Martin & Harrell, 1996, Mori, 2000). Counselors can serve as "cultural brokers" for linking students with sources of formal and informal social support on campus. Consequently, counselors need to have a campus network of resource people who demonstrate cross-cultural sensitivity and interest in international students (Siegel, 1991).

The discussion in this chapter focuses on ways to enhance direct delivery of counseling services to international students through individual or group programming. Considerations are given to the patterns of usage, overcoming barriers to accessing counseling, and practical tips for enhancing the counseling relationship with international students. When international students reach across cultural boundaries to seek counseling assistance, counselors need to be prepared to negotiate understandings about what counseling can provide, and to increase the efficacy of services for meeting international students' needs.

7.2   International Students' Use of Counseling Services

There is compelling evidence that international students underutilize counseling services, and when they do, they are often dissatisfied with the services (Pedersen, 1991). It has been suggested that international students are more likely than domestic students to drop out after a single counseling session (Anderson & Myer, 1985), however contrasting research suggests that usage rates are similar to local students (Ebbin & Blankinship, 1986) and usage rates vary according to nationality (Flathman, Davidson, & Sanford, 2001; Walker, 1999). There are several possible explanations for low usage rates of counseling services by international students. One explanation is that international students are more comfortable approaching co-nationals or their instructors if they require assistance with problem solving. However, some international students would prefer to access counseling services so that their issues are separated from their social network of academic program (Leong & Sedlacek, 1986). When students are looking for help with specific demands, a single session of counseling may meet their immediate needs. Research on usage patterns underscores the importance of counselors making the most of a single session to provide resources, support, and symptom relief from the stress associated with transition demands.

7.2.1   Counseling Styles

It has also been suggested that counseling styles have an influence on whether or not international students continue to engage with counseling services. The counseling literature generally portrays the importance of direct versus indirect methods with international students, and particularly with Asian students (Leong & Sadlacek, 1986; May & Jepsen, 1988). Yet, there is danger in stereotyping students through basing counseling styles on preconceptions. Research on counseling styles with international students is typically based on single session observations and the use of analogue simulations (e.g., D'Rozario & Romano, 2000). Comparisons are made between North American students and international students, as if both are homogeneous groups. These methodological concerns underscore the need for caution in drawing conclusions about the counseling style preferences of any group of students. Changes in the counseling process, including counseling style preferences, may shift as sessions unfold (Yau, Sue, & Hayden, 1992) and as students gain a higher comfort level and increased understanding of the counseling process. Counselors also need to consider the varying levels of acculturation held by international students to their home and host cultures (Grieger & Ponterotto, 1992).

7.2.1.1 Views towards Counselors

International students' views of counselors also influence their use and satisfaction with counseling services. Views of counselors are on a continuum ranging from authority with strong emphasis on directive and concrete advice and less emphasis on the relationship, i.e., counsellor as expert, to an informal view of the helper with a strong emphasis on the relationship, i.e., counsellor as friend (May & Jepsen, 1988). The counseling relationship is strongly influenced by international students' previous experience with hierarchical relationships (Mori, 2000). Adherence to traditional beliefs about authority and formal relationships is related to some international students' preferences for more directive and formal interactions with counselors. It is easy to see how counselors whose style is less direct and more informal are perceived as "unhelpful" by international students who view counselors as people in authority who should provide concrete advice. However, there is contrasting evidence that some groups of international students may prefer a nondirective style of counsellor expertise (D'Rozario & Romano, 2000). As international students gain experience with a host culture, their preferences for professional relationships may also change from directive to more collaborative approaches. The research on international students' preference for counseling styles remains inconclusive. What can be gleaned from this limited body of research is the importance of flexibility when counselors work with international students. Counselors must be prepared to quickly assess students' levels of acculturation and match their counseling styles, accordingly (Zhang, 1998). This is paramount during the initial counseling appointment, until rapport is established sufficiently to explore options for working together. Some students may prefer a more directive style than is typically emphasized in Western paradigms of counseling. International students want more than to be listened to; they seek solutions and suggestions for immediate concerns (Thomas & Althen, 1989). Counselors may feel in conflict about assuming more authoritarian and advise-giving roles when they have been trained to emphasize mutuality, collaboration and sharing power with clients. Counselors who are flexibility to adjust their style of counseling are likely to be more successful in engaging international students in the counseling process. As students feel more comfortable about the counsellor and the counseling process, styles of interacting can be discussed in an informative way to explore cultural norms about help-seeking.

7.2.2   Marketing Counseling Services

Perhaps the biggest deterrent against international students accessing counseling services remains their lack of awareness about the purpose and functions of counseling (Hayes & Lin, 1994). Information dissemination is a key factor in helping international students to become familiar with campus resources, including counseling services. Campus orientations are a key time to introduce counseling services, including the general purposes, types of issues that students can discuss with counselors, and logistical information about how services operate, including confidentiality. Personal contact with counselors during orientation can help international students feel more comfortable about accessing services. It is important to remember that for many students, seeking personal assistance from a stranger is a foreign idea (Fouad, 1991). Information alone will not guarantee that international students will access counseling services. Cultural norms for problem-solving and help-seeking can be prohibitive factors (Brinson & Kottler, 1995; Sandhu, 1994). It is important that reticence about accessing services not be misconstrued as indifference. The intense demands of an academic program and living in a new culture require considerable time and energy. Ironically, this can pose as a barrier to participating in student services programming designed to assist students.

The hesitancy of international students to seek services on their own means that it is crucial for counselors to take proactive approaches outside of the counseling office (Brinson & Kottler, 1995; Sandhu, 1995). Counselors need to be proactive about establishing a positive profile in the international student community to overcome some of the barriers for accessing counseling services. International students need information about the purpose of counseling and encouragement to access services that can enhance their personal and academic success (Arthur, 1997, 1998). International students who place a priority on their academic success feel more motivated to seek resources that they believe might enhance their academic situation. Positive experiences with a counsellor about academic matters can build rapport to discuss issues in other life areas. Counselors need to recognize the extra effort expended by international students to seek help and acknowledge these steps through responsive services (Hayes & Lin, 1994).

7.3   Negotiating Cultural Influences on Helping

It is critical that counselors take the lead to explore international students' expectations of counseling in order to negotiate a common framework from which to respond appropriately to clients (Thomas & Althen, 1989). Counselors need to remember that ways of defining problems and seeking help are bounded by cultural norms. One-on-one counseling is not a universal practice (Fouad, 1991). International students lack familiarity about what counseling services can offer them, the nature of a counseling relationship, and the ways that counseling can be linked to their transition concerns. "Pretherapy orientations" (Leong & Chou, 1996) help international students to be prepared for counseling and to maximize the benefits of this service.

7.3.1   Values Regarding Help-Seeking

Counselors need to explore values regarding seeking help, problem definition, as well as the resources and cultural practices used in their home culture of international students. As a starting point, an international student's attitudes towards seeking help pose as either a barrier or opportunity for working together (Grieger & Ponterotto, 1995). Many international students are reluctant to discuss personal or psychological difficulties with a professional (Lin & Yi, 1997; Mallinckrodt & Leong, 1992). However, the stress associated with cross-cultural transition could trigger the onset of serious mental health concerns (Leong & Chou, 1996; Clark Oropeza et al., 1991). It is very important for counselors to realize that an international student's concerns may be compounded through the personal conflicts that arise through seeking professional services (Leung, 1995; Wan et al., 1992). Students may simultaneously feel overloaded by transition demands and have overwhelming feelings of guilt, inadequacy, or betrayal about accessing help. Many international students would rather attempt to deal with their difficulties on their own because of the stigma associated with mental illness and the assumption that people who seek counseling services are not personally competent (Brinson & Kottler, 1995; Sandhu, 1994). Ironically, seeking counseling services may actually add to the sense of culture shock and stress experienced by international students! This sense of "double jeopardy" may be compounded for students whose cultural values include tight boundaries about managing issues alone or within the family unit (Aubrey, 1991; Dillard & Chisolm, 1983; McKinlay et al., 1996). A student who holds beliefs about maintaining personal control of problems or not disclosing personal concerns may not see view counseling as a viable resource, or at minimum, feel conflicted about accessing seeking professional services. Counselors must pay additional attention to issues of confidentiality, assurance about the legitimacy of seeking assistance, and help students to resolve negative feelings about going outside the family or cultural group for assistance.

7.3.2   Cultural Inquiry

Available counseling literature is a resource to support counselors to gain general knowledge about international students. It is important that counselors go beyond general information to considering the specific cultural contexts and influences on international students' concerns. As the identification and interpretation of client problems varies across cultures (Zhang, 1995), counselors need to incorporate a cultural assessment into their understanding about issues and ways of helping international students. A process of guided inquiry can help to conceptualize client concerns and be used to consider ways of incorporating international students' home culture into counseling interventions. Examples of inquiry questions include the following: How *would this problem be seen in your culture? How would other members of your family view this problem? How would you deal with this if you were in your home country? Who would help you? What do you think they would say to you? What would they do?* Following this process of inquiry, counselors can provide information to international students about how their issues would be viewed in the local culture and the types of interventions that would be available through counseling. Roles of counsellor and client, approaches to counseling, ways of conceptualizing client concerns, and the design of counseling interventions need to be made as transparent as possible. This avoids the risk of applying services that do not fit the expectations of clients or that do not fall within the clients' repertoire of acceptable paths for ameliorating concerns. Cultural inquiry about client issues helps both clients and counselors to become better informed and to negotiate preferred options for counseling interventions.

7.3.3   Cultural Norms in Counseling Practices

Working with clients from other cultures helps counselors discover how counseling practices are infused with cultural norms. It is also an opportunity to consider organizational development competencies that support access or pose barriers for international students. For example, the "50-minute hour" of a counseling appointment is a classic example of the emphasis on time management in Western culture. It is a convenient structure for office management, but international students may find it overly restrictive. Flexibility by counselors to spend more time with international students in fewer sessions may better match the needs of international students who seek assistance to manage pressing transition demands (Hayes & Lin, 1994). The setting of counseling services serves as another example of cultural influences on professional practice. Most counseling centers are located in areas on campus to afford student privacy. However, some international students may not want to make an appointment to see counselors in a formal setting and would prefer to keep contact on a more informal basis. Students may gain a lot from this sort of contact; however, it may raise another issue related to what counts as counseling. If we only consider contacts in the counselors' office as legitimate counseling services, then the scope of what is available to meet the needs of international students is unduly limited. Counselors may have to advocate to their administrators about the design, delivery, and evaluation of services offered to international students that are legitimate according to cultural norms of an educational institution.

7.4   Group Approaches to Counseling

Group counseling approaches, such as psychoeducational workshops and support groups, helps participants to exchange ideas and learn from the experiences of other international students. With a focus on instruction and learning, psychoeducational programming is an appropriate way to introduce topics related to cross-cultural transition. The premise of psychoeducational groups is to provide "cultural inoculation" for addressing transition demands commonly faced by international students. Orientation programs are an effective way to educate international students about commonly experienced adjustment concerns and student services designed to support their success. Beyond orientation programming offered at the beginning of the transition to the host country, counseling about re-entry transition can assist with the closure experience of leaving the host country (Arthur, in press; LaBrack, 1993). Students benefit from hearing about the experiences of other students, including coping strategies and resources available for managing transition demands (Arthur, in press; Wang, 1997). The collective identification of issues and strategies make the group a valuable resource in discussing ways to manage cross-cultural transitions. After participation in group approaches to counseling, international students may feel more comfortable about approaching a counsellor for more in-depth assistance on an individual basis.

7.4.1   Suggestions for Psychoeducational Workshops

Suggestions for planning and delivering a psychoeducational workshop with international students (Arthur, in press) can be adapted for specific workshop topics. A summary of considerations in the development and delivery of workshops with international students follows:

1. Counselors are encouraged to become familiar with the counseling literature on international students and cross-cultural transitions to gain general knowledge about common issues. Specific issues can be selected as the agenda to be covered during workshops.

2. Consultation with other members of a student services staff, such as international advisors is valuable for planning topics and the timing of workshops.

3. It is important to consult with identified leaders in the international student population. This can help to insure that topics are relevant, and it can also help with promotion of counseling programming to other international students. Feedback from students and staff should be used to make decisions about the topics, location, and format for workshops.

4. Counselors should consider whether workshops are organized for country-specific groups of students or whether they are targeted to the general international student population. This may be a factor when topics are customized to meet issues that emerge for specific groups or if the workshop is broader in scope.

5. The curriculum of workshops must be designed in light of culture specific or culture-general content. For example, the use of critical incidents, or vignettes, can be tailored around common issues or designed to incorporate culture-specific factors such as customs, values, conditions in the home country (Cushner & Brislin, 1997; Arthur, in press).

6. As emphasized in Chapters 3 and 4, programming for international students needs to go beyond identifying student concerns. Students attend workshops with the primary goal of learning strategies that will support their personal and academic success.

7. Evaluations of student workshops need to be conducted in ways to gather the opinions and recommendations of international students. This is a prime opportunity to hear from students about what they find to be valuable and what ideas they have for future

workshops. This offers an important feedback loop for program planning.

8. Counselors need to be prepared for the possibility that workshop participation may trigger strong emotional reactions. Counselors must be skilled facilitators in offering group programs. It is commonly assumed that because workshops are "educational", that they will not be intensely experienced by participants. This can leave facilitators unprepared for simultaneously supporting individual students and group dynamics.

In summary, group approaches to counseling international students are an effective way to introduce students to transition issues and coping strategies. Group interventions help participants to form social support from other international students and learn from each other's experiences. Finally, international students often find workshops to be a more acceptable format for seeking assistance when it is framed as an educational experience. Contact with counselors during orientation and workshop programming help to open the door for international students to make future contact with counselors.

7.5   Counselors as Cultural Therapists

In many ways, the role of counselors in working with international students can be described as a "cultural therapist" (Dei, 1992). Many of the concerns that arise for international students are directly related to their experience of cross-cultural transition. Counselors facilitate cultural learning through helping students to explore situations according to their ways of understanding from their home culture, and possible explanations from the point of view of values and practices in the host culture. To be effective, counselors must be comfortable exploring students' worldview and identifying ways that values, beliefs, and everyday behavior is contrasted in the host culture. The goal of counseling is not to encourage cultural assimilation. Many times, international students require pragmatic advice to help them make sense of interpersonal experiences. Interventions should be targeted at equipping students with skills and resources to enhance their capacity to function effectively in the host culture. Counseling needs to be centered on increasing international students' sense of self-efficacy to manage cross-cultural transition demands (Harrison et al., 1996).

7.5.1   Including Family Members

Counselors might also consider expanding counseling services to include family members of international students. Family members who accompany international students also experience cross-cultural transitions and their well-being can support or detract from academic achievement and the sense of satisfaction in the host country. This is a neglected area in the counseling literature with few resources available about ways to structure counseling services to support the family members of international students (Mori, 2000; de Verthelyi, 1996).

7.5.2   Addressing Culture Shock

Some students seek counseling services due to their experience of culture shock and overwhelming feelings that "something is wrong with me." Counselors can begin by normalizing this experience and helping students with symptom relief. This is a starting place from which to explore cultural differences and similarities and to help them reconcile cultural conflicts that they experience. Some international students feel concerned that life in the new culture does not afford them many opportunities for personal validation (Ishiyama, 1989). Other students may really like the opportunities for fuller expression that life in the new culture provides them. This may be a particular issue for women international students from countries and cultures where gender roles are tightly restricted. In some instances, international students seek counseling assistance to reconcile feelings of ambivalence about returning home to aspects of their culture that they deem to be undesirable.

7.5.3   Interpreting Cross-Cultural Communication

Counselors require effective communication skills for counseling students about transition issues, including competencies for interpreting meanings and responding in culturally appropriate ways (Pedersen & Ivey, 1993). In cases where international students may benefit from additional knowledge about practices in the local culture, counselors can take an instructional approach to teach students the meanings of communication and interpersonal dynamics in the host culture. This requires counselors to be astute at understanding situations from the point of view of international students, and to be able to analyze and describe the cultural significance of specific interactions in their own culture. Many things that are taken for granted in day-to-day interactions locally, can be a source of confusion and frustration for others who lack the context for interpreting behavior. This requires counselors to be able to "step outside" their cultural context, in order to appreciate how people unfamiliar with local practices may be impacted.

7.5.4   Making Decisions across Cultures

Counselors are advised to proceed cautiously with students around decision-making with international students. It is very important to consider the values that are embedded in matters of decision-making, explore with students how decisions would be viewed in their home culture, and who would be affected by their decision. Decisions made in one cultural context can have a major impact on roles and relationships defined by values in another cultural context (Arthur, 1998, 2000). Counselors must be careful not to impose their own values on the terms of decision-making. For example, Western culture may value individualism and autonomy to make decisions. This can be diametrically opposed to how decisions are made and carried out in collectivist cultures. There are profound implications for international students for their roles and relationships at home, if decisions made are in opposition to the values of their family and community.

7.5.5   Conflict Mediation

Counselors also require cross-cultural communication skills for conflict mediation. Counselors are often called upon as resource people to help resolve conflicts that occur between international students and other members of the educational community, i.e., roommates in residence, instructors, other students. This requires counselors to be familiar with the policies and rules of various campus areas and help both parties seek an agreement that is respectful of the institution and of each other. Conflict across cultures is complex for several reasons (Singelis & Pedersen, 1997). First, when individuals hold divergent beliefs and values, the potential for conflict escalates. Second, situations become more volatile through cultural misunderstandings and miscommunication. Third, holding onto personal interests and lack of cultural understanding contributes to barriers for identifying mutual interests and avenues for conflict resolution. Unfortunately, cross-cultural communication skills, including mediation are rarely included in the curriculum of counsellor education programs. Counselors can benefit from learning about the Interpersonal Cultural Grid (Singelis & Pedersen, 1997; Stewart, in press) as a resource for conflict mediation. The essence of this resource is moving disputes forward by recognizing how misunderstandings about behavior occur and focusing on the intent of behavior and shared positive expectations. Negotiating common ground builds a foundation from which to generate alternative solutions. Counselors who are skilled in the use of the Interpersonal Cultural Grid can help the respective parties move from a position of ethnocentrism and focus on areas of similarity and mutually beneficial actions. Both parties may be able to view the behavior of the other person in new ways that can result in cultural learning and stronger abilities to work together. If counselors are consulted early in an interpersonal conflict, they can help to resolve cultural conflict before situations move to a state where there are serious consequences for either an international student or other members of the campus community.

7.6   Language Proficiency and Counseling

Language proficiency is a key issue for international students in adjusting to life in a new country. International students with stronger language proficiency report fewer adjustment problems than students who rate themselves as having weaker language proficiency (Wan et al., 1992). Language proficiency permeates the many roles that international students enact in the new culture and impacts their capacity for cultural learning. International students often chose a foreign education for the explicit purpose of strengthening their language capacity. However, simultaneously learning a second language, managing academic demands, and establishing new interpersonal relationships takes considerable energy and can take its toll on student health. Language proficiency is critical for cultural adjustment and has been described as a parallel process called "language shock" (Smalley, 1963). Studying in a second language is extremely taxing when students must spend extra time to understand written materials and to understand verbal instruction. International students miss social cues when they do not understand the nuances of the local language. Language proficiency impacts the quality of relationships that students are able to develop in academic and social situations.

7.6.1   Language Proficiency and Individual Counseling

Language proficiency also impacts interaction between international students and counselors. Language shock emerges during counseling as both international students and counselors may feel limited about their language abilities. For example, a limited vocabulary for explaining personal concerns inhibits the level of understanding that counselors are able to gain regarding client issues. International students may have a limited vocabulary from which to present their issues and to describe associated symptoms of culture shock. Difficulties communicating with a counsellor can exacerbate a sense of anxiety or embarrassment about seeking professional services.

Conversely, counselors feel a sense of discomfort or anxiety about ways to assist international students when language proficiency is a barrier. It is important for counselors to be informed about the impact of language proficiency for students' interpersonal and academic adjustment. During a counseling session, students need reassurance to help them feel at ease. It is frustrating for students to not be able to express themselves in fuller ways. Students may have concerns about how the counsellor will perceive them. Counselors who express sincere concern about wanting to help students and who are able to help contribute to the quality of the conversation will help students overcome language barriers (Hays & Lin, 1994). Counselors can encourage clients to take the time they need to formulate their words, offer words to help with explanations, and include lots of paraphrasing and perception checking to insure they understand their clients. Although students may feel limited about expressing themselves in a second language, counselors can often assure them through humor; international students are likely more proficient in speaking the counsellor's first language than vice-versa!

7.6.2   Language Proficiency and Group Counseling

Language proficiency also surfaces as an issue during group approaches to counseling with international students (Arthur, in press). When counselors facilitate groups, norms should be introduced about language use. This includes whether discussion between students is allowed or encouraged, or whether or not students can work together on assigned tasks. It is useful to have a resource person attend the workshop who is fluent in participants' first language. There are benefits for students from accessing translation of key words and phrases as the workshop progresses. Norms for discussion between students in their first language also need to be negotiated, in order to create a level of comfort for all participants. This saves misunderstandings about why students are talking together and helps students who have difficulties with language to feel more comfortable coming forward for assistance. Side conversations during a workshop can be a distraction for the facilitator and for other participants. However, if participants have a common understanding of their supportive value, minor disruptions are tolerated to enhance learning for international students. This also requires counselors to examine their personal comfort levels about how communication patterns transpire during the delivery of workshops. Counselors may have beliefs that learning must take place in a quiet and controlled atmosphere. This is contrary to the actual needs of many international students for interruptions to the flow of information for clarification, the ability to confer with colleagues, and more than one or two people talking at once. Counselors can feel confident about creating a workshop environment that supports international students with their learning needs.

7.7 Helping Students Manage Their Views of Cross-Cultural Transition

Through the process of acculturation, international students often shift their views about both the host and home culture. This can be experienced akin to an emotional roller coaster, with fluctuations about the excitement and novelty of the new culture, feeling overwhelmed by cultural learning, and missing the familiarity of life at home. International students typically engage in an ongoing comparison of their home and host cultures as students experience cultural contrasts. Comparison is also a way for students to processing their learning about culture. However, this comparison can become problematic when students dichotomize their experiences. This can lead to "all or nothing" comparisons, in which home and host cultures are subsequently labeled as "good" or "bad." Counselors need to consider the influences of acculturation on presenting client issues (Grieger & Ponterotto, 1995). It may be helpful to explore students' evaluations of how they are coping in the host culture. When culture shock is experienced as a strong reaction, students may jump to the conclusion that they are not managing anything well.

7.7.1 Keeping Cultural Learning in Sight

Although the original models of culture shock have their limitations, as discussed in Chapter 2, they have heuristic value for illustrating to the students the "ups and downs" of cross-cultural transition (Arthur, in press). Discussion of cross-cultural transition can be introduced through showing students a picture of the W-curve model of culture shock (Gullahorn & Gullahorn, 1963). Counselors can encourage students to identify specific aspects of their cross-cultural transition, i.e., academic program, making new friends, trying new food, speaking a second language, etc. and map their progress. It is important to help students reframe their experiences in specific terms so that they can keep sight of transition demands that they are mastering and those that require additional coping skills. Counselors can support this process through teaching students about characteristics of transition (Schossberg, 1984) or helping them to complete a validationgram exercise (Ishiyama, 1989, 1995) that identifies specific domains of cross-cultural transition. The goal of counseling is not eliminate culture shock, rather, to help students to alleviate symptoms so that they are able to continue to engage in the process of cultural learning. Students might also find journaling to be a useful technique for identifying critical events in their cross-cultural experience and for reflecting about how well they are coping (Arthur, 2001). These techniques are examples of ways that counselors can support international students to be reflect about transition demands, identify their progress in mastering aspects of the local culture, and to identify specific areas where counseling interventions may be implemented.

7.8   Ethical Issues

Counseling international students can challenge notions of ethical practice. It is not uncommon for situations to emerge that contravene or diverge from "textbook practices" in counsellor education programs. Counselors may feel torn between following ethical practices that they have been taught and losing international students as a client, or alternatively, practicing in ways with international student clients that violate codes of ethical conduct. Counselors who work with culturally diverse clients need to be flexible in their practices and consider ways to best deliver counseling services. This requires sorting out ethical principles that are "fundamental" to professional practices and cannot be modified, and those that are "discretionary" practices that can be adapted to specific settings and to specific clients (Pedersen, 1995).

As a starting point, counselors should become familiar with their respective professional codes of ethics, paying particular attention to the recommendations for practice with clients who are culturally diverse. It is noteworthy that codes of ethics are constructed in a particular cultural context and, consequently, they reflect the assumptions of that context (Pedersen, 1997). Counselors are encouraged to become familiar with the debates surrounding the application of ethical principles in different cultures. Reviewing the literature on ethical practices with clients who are culturally diverse can help counselors to identify key issues and solutions in multicultural counseling (e.g., LaFromboise, Foster, & James, 1996; Pedersen, 1995, 1997; Pettifor, 2001; Ridley, Liddle, Hill, & Li, 2001).

7.8.1   Professional Competence

There are several areas of professional practice where ethical issues may surface in counseling international students. As discussed in Chapter 5, there are professional imperatives directed towards counselors to be competent for working across cultures. Although counselors may receive general training about multicultural counseling, specific knowledge and practices for working with international students are rarely included in counsellor education programs. This requires counselors to seek out information about this population and to establish a network of resource people on campus who can serve as consultants for working with international students. Counselors should also consider receiving supervision with a supervisor trained in multicultural counseling about cases involving international students (Dillard & Chisolm, 1983). This is a wonderful opportunity for both supervisors and counselors to examine multicultural issues in supervision, paying specific attention to the potential influences of culture on the counsellor-client dyad (Brown & Landrum-Brown, 1995; Chen, 2001). Supervision can help counselors to engage in a "cultural audit" of their practices with clients, including the conceptualization of problems, dynamics in building a therapeutic alliance, and in selecting and implementing counseling interventions. In order to stay abreast of "what works" in counseling international students, counselors should invite students to evaluate their services.

7.8.2   Boundary Issues

International students' views of the counsellor may pose ethical dilemmas. This usually surfaces as a boundary issues and concern about dual roles. It is generally supported in the counseling literature that counselors need to take extra steps to gain a positive profile in the international student community on campus. It is also suggested that counselors participate in student orientations and the delivery of psychoeducational workshops. This increases the chances that counselors have contact with international students in more than one context and in more than one role. What should be discussed in a social or workshop context in comparison to an individual counseling session may not be clearly defined, in fact, some international students may not see the need to separate these contexts at all. Due to the strong need and appreciation for social support, it is easy for international students to define their relationships with counselors as going beyond a professional context. When a counsellor is one of few sources of social support, there may be requests for meeting and time spent together outside of the counseling role. Again, cultural values may explain these circumstances. Someone who is helpful may be viewed not only as an authority figure, but more like a close friend. It may be confusing for international students that counselors are not interested or available to pursue interaction beyond defined campus roles. To avoid offending students and to avoid potential role conflicts, counselors must be prepared to explain the limits of their relationships with international students. Although this may be disappointing for some international students, it can also be instructive about professional practices in the local culture. Counselors should focus on helping international students to build stronger social connections and a wider repertoire of people in their social network.

7.8.3   Exchanging Gifts

The giving and receiving of gifts is another area that is often contentious in counseling relationships. In many cultures around the world, gift giving is a common practice to express appreciation. Not accepting a gift could be viewed as highly offensive to the point of severing a relationship. Counselors must carefully consider the intent and potential meanings associated to gift giving by international students. Some counseling offices have adopted a "no gifts" policy as a uniform way of managing this area of ethical practice. This type of policy does not incorporate culture views of gift giving as social courtesy and sign of respect and appreciation. However, the meaning of gift giving may also extend into more risky areas for professional practice due to cultural expectations for returning favors through securing a sense of obligation. Each situation requires a judgment call on behalf of the counsellor in weighing the potential risks and benefits for the individual client, for the counsellor, and for professional practice.

7.8.4   Confidentiality

Issues of confidentiality are paramount in any counseling relationship. As discussed earlier in this chapter, international students may have heightened anxiety about seeking professional counseling services due to the perceived stigma, or due to cultural restraints about discussing personal matters outside of their family or cultural group. International students require extra attention in discussing the terms of confidentiality, particularly information about who has access to the information that they share with a counsellor. Another concern that must be addressed is any potential link between counseling services and students' academic programs. Students may need assurances that they will not "get into trouble" by discussing academic concerns. Some students may welcome the privacy and formality of counseling services, to avoid identification by others. Alternatively, some students may stretch counselors' views about privacy and confidentiality and openly share information about what transpires in counseling with others. Students from collective cultures may prefer to have one or more friends accompanying them to a counseling session, or they may present as a group. Alternatively, a representative of an international student group may also approach a counsellor on behalf of the issues experienced by other students. This can be a way of "checking out the counsellor" and assessing whether or not the service seems to be a useful resource. In every interaction with international students, counselors leave an impression that will be passed along to other students about their approachability and the usefulness of counseling as a campus resource.

7.9   Future Directions in Counseling International Students

International students are a culturally diverse population of students. We are just beginning to understand the complex ways in which culture influences international students' experience of transition. The counseling literature is limited in the ways that international students are portrayed, and consequently, our understanding of how counseling services can be responsive to their needs is compromised. Several areas are suggested for future research and program planning with international students.

7.9.1   Expanding Perspectives about Cross-Cultural Transition

Four areas within the counseling literature have been identified that contribute to the marginalization of international students (Popadiuk & Arthur, in press). First, the early models of culture shock need to be augmented in their explanation of cross-cultural transition. Although the U-curve (Lysgaard, 1955) and W-curve (Gullahorn & Gullahorn, 1963) models alerted us to the shifting nature of transitions over culture, they are inadequate to account for the experiences of international students. For example, culture shock has primarily been portrayed as a negative experience and a maladaptive response to cultural contrasts. When culture shock is viewed this way, as something to be avoided or as a "disease", the implication is to eradicate it or avoid culture shock. Another implication is to let students "run the course of the 'culture shock cycle' and once 'adjusted' they 'recover' as if they have had a cold or the flu" (McKinlay et al.; Gross, 1996). A contrasting view sees culture shock as an inevitable process, determined by the extent to which students face contrasts between the home and host cultures. Rather than viewing culture shock as a negative reaction, it can be seen as a positive motivator for cultural learning. International students choose to study in a foreign country to learn about new ways of understanding the world. Culture shock is a process through which students come to understand aspects of their new environment, and face new understandings about aspects of their home culture. Often, the need for rapid cultural learning is most apparent at the initial stage of contact with a new culture. The need for cultural learning fluctuates as new demands are perceived and others are managed over time (Arthur, 1997; Shougee, 1999). It is not advisable to consider the whole transition experience as an entire entity; rather aspects of the experience, as students master demands and face new ones that fluctuate over time. Rather than viewing culture shock in such a negative light, it needs to be associated with cultural learning and as a necessary process in the experience of cross-cultural transition (Huxur et al., 1996).

Alternatively, counselors need to expand their repertoire of understanding about cross-cultural transition through examining a variety of models. The complexity of cross-cultural transitions and the adjustment of international students are better understood as processes of acculturation (Berry, 1997, 2001) and enculturation. The concepts of internationalized or subjective culture are important for understanding people's experience of cross-cultural transition. In a lovely metaphor, Draguns (1996) notes that our subjective culture is like the air that we breathe, and it only when we are deprived of it, that we notice it. Similarly, it is only when international students are deprived of the home culture that they have internalized that they become aware of the influence on them. This is a good reminder for counselors to remember that international students' experiences about culture shock may be related to increasing awareness and learning about their own culture, as well as new learning about the host culture. Ho's (1995) definition of the enculturation process is useful for explaining "how people are actually exposed to, learn from, and are influenced by the culture to which they are exposed" (p. 5). This model helps counselors to appreciate the individual differences in reactions between international students from the same culture.

7.9.2   Reciprocal Learning in Cross-Cultural Transition

A second concern with the counseling literature on international students is the focus on individual adaptation. The risk is that the onus for adjustment, including academic and personal success, is placed in the individual student. This ignores vital dynamics in the reciprocal interactions between members of the host culture and international students. Counselors need to familiar with acculturation, which accounts for the process that occurs when members of two or more cultural groups come into contact with each other, with the potential for cultural learning (Casas, 1995). Acculturation is considered to be both unidirectional and bi-directional (Berry, 1997, 2001; Sodowsky & Plake, 1992). Unidirectional acculturation occurs when the onus is placed on international students to assimilate into the practices of the host culture. In contrast, when the process is bi-directional, there are higher degrees of commitment from members of the host culture to learn about international students and their cultures. A difficult question might be asked: "To what extent are members of campus communities prepared to engage in bi-directional learning?" This question must also be asked about counselors and the services that they represent. The responsiveness of the host culture, including counselors, influences whether the onus stays with international students to "sink or swim" as they navigate the new culture, or whether services can be designed to facilitate new learning and understanding by members of both cultures. Counselors benefit from gaining a broader conceptualization of the dynamics of cross-cultural transition. Future directions in counseling international students would focus on identifying ways to offer counseling services to students that would engage them willingly and not feel like they are accessing a "foreign service." Additionally, counselors can help to facilitate campus programming with faculty and local students through encouraging them to build meaningful relationships with international students.

7.9.3   Expanding Research Methodology

A third concern pertains to generalization in the counseling literature about international students. The literature provides an overall sense of the common issues faced by international students; however, it tends to be superficial and stereotypes students as if they all had the same experiences (Popadiuk & Arthur, in press). The risk is that counselors may adopt stereotypical assumptions about international students and not seek to understand the uniqueness of issues and circumstances that individual students experience. Part of what contributes to the "homogenization" of international students is the way that the majority of research has been conducted. General information about international students dominates the counseling literature because the vast majority of research has been conducted using quantitative methods such as survey research (Bontrager, Birch, & Kracht, 1990; Mallinckrodt & Leong, 1992; Parr et al., 1992). The results of this type of research are certainly useful as a starting point for appreciating the common experiences of international students. However, it does not contribute to counselors' understanding about the complex influences of cultural diversity in students' backgrounds, the diverse experiences they face during cross-cultural transition, and directions for addressing the unique needs that students may present to counseling services (Popadiuk & Arthur, in press, Pedersen, 1991). The intersection of cultural dimensions such as gender, race, and religion, are obscured is obscured by aggregate research methods. As an alternative, some researchers are focusing on specific groups of international students, especially Asian students (e.g., Kwan, Sodowsky, & Ihle, 1994; Liberman, 1994; Lin & Yi, 1997; Yang, Teraoka, Eichenfield, & Audas, 1994). At first glance, this may appear as a step forward, in an exploration of the particular subgroups of the international student population. However, even these studies appear to reduce students to a group identity, and do not take into consideration the vast cultural diversity within a population categorized as "Asian." Unfortunately, stereotypes may inadvertently be perpetuated. The counseling literature tends to make this subgroup of international students appear more homogeneous than they are in reality (Popadiuk & Arthur, in press).

Qualitative methodologies are emerging in research through efforts to give voice to the individual experiences and personal perspectives of international students (e.g., Brinson & Kottler, 1995; Han, Jamieson, & Young, 2000; Huzur et al., 1996; Pedersen, 1995a; Shougee, 1999). Research methodology such as semi-structured interviews offers a focus on specific issue, while allowing the unique experiences of international students to be heard. As methodologies in qualitative research gain popularity, methods such as in-depth interpretive inquiries could complement existing research and expand our points of view about the experiences of international students (Popadiuk & Arthur, in press). Needs assessment with international students using a variety of methodologies, such as surveys with open-ended questions and focus groups help determine the degree to which existing programs and services address student needs (Luzzo & Henao, 1996).

7.9.4   Shifting from Problems to Strengths and Resources

A fourth issue pertains to focus on problems faced by students in adapting to life in a new country. To date, research has primarily focused on their problems and concerns but has not been balanced with the same efforts to research international students' strengths and coping resources. The resiliency of international students is frequently referred to in passing, but not substantiated by the direction of researchers' agendas. Platitudes and praise for international students, such their "courage, initiatives, and ambitions...deserve unqualified admiration and praise"...(Sandhu, 1994, p. 230), however complimentary, are not a substitute for research-based inquiry into students' experiences of positive adaptation (Popadiuk & Arthur, in press). In summarizing the research on international students and their concerns, the conclusion that these students are "rather robust" (Parr et al., 1992) implies the wide range of experiences and personal attributes that are more positive than negative.

The pleasant experiences of international students and their personal and educational goal attainments are rarely noted in literature pertaining to their mental health (Sandhu & Asrabadi, 1994). Whereas the major concerns of mental health practitioners and counselors may be on problematic issues of adjustment, caution should be given against viewing international students as a "problematic" population. Agendas that are focused on problems give the implicit message that international students are problem-laden (Popadiuk & Arthur, in press). This ignores the major contributions that international students make to the internationalization of educational institutions (Arthur, 1997). Several of these contributions were summarized in Chapter 1. Beyond economic contributions, international students also contribute to the development of international alumni, provide networking opportunities for future student recruitment, and build longer-term international relations for the export of educational curriculum (Dei, 1992; Diambomba, 1993; Francis, 1993). Familiarity with the positive experiences and accomplishments of international students can help to balance perspectives about this population.

7.9.5   Re-Entry and Integrating International Experience

Research on international students has also been imbalanced by the continued emphasis on the initial stage of transition, without due consideration of the longer-term issues of adjustment that occur in cross-cultural transition. In particular, there is very little research addressing the stage of re-entry transition. Further research is needed to appreciate the issues faced by international students as they depart from the host country and return to life at home. This is surprising, given that one of the unique characteristics of this population is that they are temporary residents and the transition home is an inevitable outcome of the experience of becoming an international student. The discussion in Chapter 4 outlines the variety of issues that international students face as they disengage from their life in a foreign country and return to life at home. Again, research needs to extend from a problem-focus to considering the coping strategies that help international students manage the issues that surface in the re-entry transition. Ultimately, students take their international experience home. Counselors need to know more about how international students integrate their international experience into personal and professional development (Arthur, 2002, in press).

7.10   Concluding Comments

Growing opportunities for student mobility through international education means that support services on campus must keep pace. Efforts to recruit more international students have implications for campus infrastructure. Counselors could play a stronger role in helping international students successfully integrate into local school and community environments. This requires a systematic approach to designing counseling services that are responsive to the issues that international students face during cross-cultural transition. Counselors need to be familiar with models of cross-cultural transition to appreciate the demands that impinge upon students as they navigate new ways of learning and living in a new culture. International students are a unique population in that their time in the host culture is temporary. Their experiences can prompt learning through exposure to new values, beliefs, educational practices, and ways of interacting socially. For some international students, cultural learning prompts considerable dissonance as they attempt to reconcile aspects of their home culture with new practices. For other international students, cultural learning helps them to gain a stronger sense of appreciation about the strengths of their home culture. The experience of cross-cultural transition prompts changes in the ways that international students view themselves, other people, and the world around them.

Counselors who work in educational institutions need to be informed about the issues that international students experience during cross-cultural transition. Counselors' main responsibilities are working directly with students in ways that help them problem-solve transition issues and develop effective coping skills. However, the responsibilities of counselors need to be broadened to include advocacy and educational roles that foster a supportive campus environment for international students. Counselors also have a role to play as consultants and resource people in the development and design of orientation and psychoeducational workshops to address student needs. Counselors' roles in the larger campus community can include advocacy to promote campus internationalization and overcome systemic and organizational barriers that negatively impact international students.

Counseling services need to be systematically organized and adapted in ways to provide effective outreach services. Beyond taking a personal interest in this student population, counselors need to have multicultural counseling competencies. Inevitably, counseling international students means working across cultures. This can be an opportunity for counselors to seriously examine the influences of culture on clients' presenting issues, the impact of culture in the counsellor-client relationship, and to explore interventions that are culturally meaningful to clients. International students can also challenge counselors to examine their beliefs about how counseling should unfold and to examine their notions about "what counts" as counseling.

The population of international students encompasses many countries and many cultures from around the world. Counselors need to consider both the general needs and unique circumstances of international clients, and assess their individual strengths and resources. Working with international students affords counselors the opportunity to practice and enhance their multicultural counseling competencies. Counselors who take a genuine interest in international students will inevitably be rewarded with rich cultural learning about student experiences and the process of cross-cultural transition. In turn, international students will receive the recognition that they deserve with support to navigate the academic and personal demands of living and learning in a new culture.

Counseling international students affords opportunities for working with clients from around the world. From this experience both clients and counselors can learn about new ways of viewing the world.

References

Achenbach, K., & Arthur, N. (2002). Experiential learning: Bridging theory to practice in multicultural counseling. *Guidance & Counseling, 17,* 39-45.

Adler, N.J. (1981). Re-entry: Managing cross-cultural transitions. *Group and Organizational Studies, 6,* 341-356.

Aigner, J.S., Nelson, P., & Stimpfl, J. (1992). *Internationalizing the University: Making it work.* Springfield, VA: CBIS Federal Inc.

Akande, A. (1994). The international students at the University of Ibadan. *International Journal of Adolescence and Youth, 5,* 127-138.

Alexander, M. A., & Shaw, E. (1991). International students at a College of Nursing: Concerns and coping. *Journal of American College Health, 39,* 245-247.

American Counseling Association. (1995). *Code of ethics and standards of practice.* Alexandria, VA: Author.

Anderson, T., & Myer, T. (1985). Presenting problems, counselor contacts, and "no shows": International and American college students. *Journal of College Student Personnel, 26,* 500-503.

Arredondo, P., Toropek, R., Brown, S.P., Jones, J., Locke, D.C., Sanchez, J., & Stadler, H. (1996). Operationalization of the multicultural counseling competencies. *Journal of Multicultural Counseling and Development, 24,* 42-78.

Arthur, N. (1995). International training: The new realities of doing business internationally. *ACCC Community, 18,* 9.

Arthur, N. (1997). Counseling international students. *Canadian Journal of Counseling, 31,* 259-274.

Arthur, N. (1998). Intergenerational conflict in career and life planning. *National consultation on career development- NATCON papers - 24* (pp. 95-104). Toronto, ON: OISE Press.

Arthur, N. (2000a). Preparing globally minded students and employees. *National consultation on career development – NATCON papers- 26,* pp. 1-10. Retrieved April 15, 2003, from http://www.contactpoint.ca/html/natcon-conat/2000/abs/abs-00-16.html

Arthur, N. (2000b). Career competencies for managing cross-cultural transitions. *Canadian Journal of Counseling, 34,* 204-217.

Arthur, N. (2001). Using critical incidents to investigate cross-cultural transitions. *International Journal of Intercultural Relations, 25*, 41-53.

Arthur, N. (2002). Preparing students for a world of work in cross-cultural transition. *Australian Journal of Career Development, 11*(1), 9-13.

Arthur, N. (2003). Preparing international students for the re-entry transition. *Canadian Journal of Counselling, 37* (3), 173-185.

Arthur, N., & Hayward, L. (1997). The relationships between perfectionism, standards for academic achievement, and emotional distress in postsecondary students. *Journal of College Student Development, 38*, 622-633.

Arthur, N. & Hiebert, B. (1996). Coping with the transition to post-secondary education. *Canadian Journal of Counseling, 2*, 93-103.

Arthur, N., & Stewart, J. (2001). Multicultural counseling in the new millennium: Introduction to the special theme issue. *Canadian Journal of Counseling, 35, 3-14.*

Aspland, T. (1999). *Speaking about supervision: A study of thesis supervision for overseas women students enrolled in doctoral programs in Australian universities.* Non-published dissertation. University of Queensland.

Association of Universities and Colleges of Canada. (2003). *International student recruitment- AUCC background document.* Ottawa, ON: Author.

Atkinson, D.R., Morten, G., & Sue, D.W. (1989). A minority identity development model. In D.R. Atkinson, G. Morten, & D.W. Sue (Eds.), *Counseling American Minorities* (pp. 35-52). Dubuque, IA: W.C. Brown.

Atkinson, D.R., Thompson, C.E., & Grant, S.K. (1993). A three-dimensional model for counseling racial/ethinic minorities. *Counseling Psychologist, 21, 257-277.*

Aubrey, R. (1991). International students on campus: A challenge for counselors, medical providers, and clinicians. *Smith College Studies in Social Work, 62*(1), 20-33.

Australian Education International (2001). *Overseas student statistics.* Canberra, ACT: Department of Education, Science and Training.

Axelson, J.A. (1999). *Counseling and development in a multicultural society* (3rd ed.). Toronto, ON: Brooks/Cole.

Bagley, C.A., & Copeland, E.J., (1994). African and African American graduate students' racial identity and personal problem-solving strategies. *Journal of Counseling & Development, 73, 168-171*

Baptiste, D., (1990). The treatment of adolescents and their families in cultural transition: Issues and recommendations. *Contemporary Family Therapy, 12*(1), 3-22.

Baptiste, D. (1993). Immigrant families, adolescents and acculturation: Insights for therapists. *Marriage and Family Review, 19*, 341-363.

Barker, M., Child, C., Gallois, C., Jones, E., & Callan, V.J. (1991). Difficulties of overseas students in social and academic situations. *Australian Journal of Psychology, 43*(2), 79-84.

Berry, J.W. (1984). Psychological adaptation of foreign students. In R. Samuda & A. Wolfgang (Eds.), *Intercultural counseling and assessment* (pp. 235-248). Toronto, ON: Hogrefe.

Berry, J.W. (1997). Immigration, acculturation, and adaptation. *Applied Psychology: An International Review, 46*(1), 5-68.

Berry, J.W. (2001). A psychology of immigration. *Journal of Social Issues, 57*, 615-631.

Berry, J.W. & Kim, U. (1988). Acculturation and mental health. In P.R. Dasen, J.W., Berry, & N. Sartorius (Eds.), *Health and cross-cultural psychology: Towards applications* (pp. 207-238). Newbury Park, CA: Sage.

Berry, J.W., Kim, U., Mindle, T., & Mok, D. (1987). Comparative studies of acculturative stress. *International Migration Review, 21*, 491-511.

Bikos, L. H., & Furry, T. S. (1999). The Job Search Club for international students: An evaluation. *The Career Development Quarterly, 48*, 31-44.

Bochner, S., Hutnik, N., & Furnham, A. (1985). The friendship patterns of overseas and host students in an Oxford student residence. *The Journal of Social Psychology, 125*, 689-694.

Bohm, A., Davis, D., Meares, D., & Pearce, D. (2002). *Global student mobility 2025: Forecasts of the global demand for international higher education.* Sydney, NSW: IDP Education Australia

Bontrager, T., Birch, W. G., & Kracht, J. B. (1990). International students' concerns: Directions of supportive programming. *The College Student Affairs Journal, 10*(2), 22-28.

Brabant, S., Palmer, C.E., & Gramling, R. (1990). Returning home: An empirical investigation of cross-cultural reentry. *International Journal of Intercultural Relations, 14*, 387-404.

Brammer, L., & Abrego, P. (1981). Intervention strategies for coping with transitions. *The Counseling Psychologist, 9*(2), 19-36.

Brammer, L., & Abrego, P. (1992). Counseling adults for career change. In H. D. Lea & Z.B. Leibowitz (Eds.), *Adult career development: Concepts, issues, and practices* (2nd Ed.), (pp. 90-101). Alexandria, VA: National Career Development Association.

Bridges, W. (1991). *Managing transitions: Making the most of change.* Reading, MA: Addison-Wesley.

Brinson, J. A., & Kottler, J. (1995). International students in counseling: Some alternative models. *Journal of College Student Psychotherapy, 9*(3), 57-70.

Brookfield, S. (1995). *Becoming a critically reflective practitioner.* Thousand Oaks, CA: Sage.

Brown, M.T., & Landrum-Brown, J. (1995). Counselor supervision: cross-cultural perspectives. In J.G. Ponterotto, J.M. Casas, L.A. Suzuki, L.A., & C.M. Alexander (Eds.), *Handbook of multicultural counseling* (pp. 263-286). Thousand Oaks, CA: Sage.

Canadian Bureau for International Education (1997). *The national report of international students in Canada, 1996/97.* Ottawa, ON: Author.

Canadian Bureau for International Education (2002). *The national report of international students in Canada, 2000/01.* Ottawa, ON: Author.

Canadian Psychological Association. (1996). *Guidelines for non-discriminatory practice.* Ottawa, ON: Author.

Casas, J. M. (1995). Counseling and psychotherapy with racial/ethnic minority groups in theory and practice. In B. Bongar & L. E. Beutler (Eds.), *Comprehensive textbook of psychotherapy: Theory and practice* (pp. 311-335). New York: Oxford University Press

Casas, J.M., & Pytluk, S.D. (1995). Hispanic identity development. In J.G. Ponterotto, J.M. Casas, L.A. Suzuki, L.A., & C.M. Alexander (Eds.), *Handbook of multicultural counseling* (pp. 155-180). Thousand Oaks, CA: Sage.

Chen, C.P. (1999). Common stressors among international college students: research and counseling implications. *Journal of College Counseling, 2*, 49-65.

Chen, E.C. (2001). Multicultural counseling supervision: An interactional approach. In J.G. Ponterotto, J.M. Casas, L.A. Suzuki, L.A., & C.M. Alexander (Eds.), *Handbook of multicultural counseling* (2nd ed.) (pp. 801-824). Thousand Oaks, CA: Sage.

Chin, H.K. (2002). *Open doors: Report on international educational exchange.* New York, NY: Institute of International Education.

Church, A.T. (1982). Sojourner adjustment. *Psychological Bulletin, 91,* 540-572. Clark Oropeza, B.A., Fitzgibbon, M., & Baron, A. (1991). Managing mental health crises of foreign college students. *Journal of Counseling & Development, 69,* 280-284.

Collingridge, D. S. (1999). Suggestions on teaching international students: Advice for psychology instructors. *Teaching of Psychology, 26*(2), 126-128.

Cownie, F., & Addison, W. (1996). International students and language support: A new survey. *Studies in Higher Education, 21,* 221-231.

Crano, S.L., & Crano, W.D. (1993). A measure of adjustment strain in international students. *Journal of Cross-Cultural Psychology, 24*, 267-283. Cross, S.E. (1995). Self-construals, coping, and stress in cross-cultural adaptation. *Journal of Cross-Cultural Psychology, 26*, 673-697.

Cross, S.E. (1995). The psychology of Nigrescence: Revisiting the Cross model. In J.G. Ponterotto, J.M. Casas, L.A. Suzuki, L.A., & C.M. Alexander (Eds.), *Handbook of multicultural counseling* (pp. 93-122). Thousand Oaks, CA: Sage.

Cunningham, C.G. (1991). *The integration of international students on Canadian post-secondary campuses.* Ottawa, ON: Canadian Bureau for International Education.

Cushner, K., & Brislin, W. (1997). Key concepts in the field of cross-cultural training: An introduction. In K. Cushner & W. Brislin (Eds.), *Improving intercultural interactions: Modules for cross-cultural training programs Volume 2* (pp. 1-20). Thousand Oaks, CA: Sage.

Dadfar, S., & Friedlander, M.L. (1982). Differential attitudes of international students toward seeking professional psychological help. *Journal of Counseling Psychology, 29*, 335-338.

Dana, R. (1998). *Understanding cultural identity in intervention and assessment.* Thousand Oaks, CA: Sage.

Davis, T. (1997). *Open doors 1996/97: Report on international educational exchange.* New York, NY: Institute of International Education.

Davis, T. (2001). *Open doors 2000/01: Report on international educational exchange.* New York, NY: Institute of International Education.

Dei, G.J. (1992). *The social reality of international post-secondary students in Canada.* Ottawa, Ontario: Canadian Bureau for International Education.

de Verthelyi, R. (1996). Facilitating cross-cultural adjustment: a newsletter by and for international students' spouses. *Journal of College Student Development, 37*, 699-701.

Diambomba, M. (1993). *Economic impact of international students in Canada: Exploratory cost-benefit analysis.* Ottawa, Ontario: Canadian Bureau for International Education.

Dillard, J. M., & Chisolm, G. B. (1983). Counseling the international student in a multicultural context. *Journal of College Student Personnel, 24*(2), 101-105.

Draguns, J. G. (1996). Humanly universal and culturally distinctive: Charting the course of cultural counseling. In P. B. Pedersen & J. G. Draguns & W. J. Lonner & J. E. Trimble (Eds.), *Counseling Across Cultures*

(4th ed.) (pp. 1-20). Thousand Oaks, CA: Sage.

D'Rozario, V, Ebbin, A.J., & Blankinship, E.S. (1986). A longitudinal health care study: International versus domestic students. *Journal of American College Health, 34*, 177-182.

D'Rozario, V., & Romano, J.L. (2000). Perceptions of counselor effectiveness: A study of two country groups. *Counseling Psychology Quarterly, 13, 51-63.*

Essandoh, P. K. (1996). Multicultural counseling as the "fourth force": A call to arms. *The Counseling Psychologist, 24*, 126-137.

Fouad, N.A. (1991). Training counselors to counsel international students: Are we ready? *The Counseling Psychologist, 19,* 66-71.

Flathman, O.Y., Davidson, M., & Sanford, T. (2001, March). *International students at American counseling centers: A study of utilization patterns.* Poster presented at the Division 17 Counseling Psychology Conference, Houston, Texas.

Flett, G.L., Blankstein, K., Hewitt, P.L. & Koledin, S. (1992). Components of perfectionism and procrastination in college students. *Social Behaviour and Personality, 20,* 85-94.

Francis, A. (1993). *Facing the future: The internationalization of post-secondary institutions in British Columbia.* Vancouver, British Columbia: British Columbia Centre for Education.

Fukuyama, M.A., & Sevig, T.D. (1999). *Integrating spirituality into multicultural counseling.* Thousand Oaks, CA: Sage.

Furnham & Alibhai, N. (1985). The friendship networks of foreign students: A replication and extension of the functional model. *International Journal of Psychology, 20*, 709-722.

Furnham, A., & Bochner, S. (1986). *Culture shock: Psychological reactions to unfamiliar environments.* London: Methuen.

Gaw, K.F. (2000). Reverse culture shock in students returning from overseas. International *Journal of Intercultural Relations, 24*, 83-104.

Gibbons, J.L., Stiles, D. A., & Shkodriani, G.M. (1991). Adolescents' attitudes toward family and gender roles: An international comparison. *Sex Roles, 25*, 625-643.

Greenberg, D. (2003). U.S. screening system for foreign students criticized. *Lancet, 361*(9365), 1280.

Greenwood, A.W., & Westwood, M.J. (1991). *Returning home: Leader's manual.* Ottawa, ON: Canadian Bureau for International Education.

Grieger, I., & Ponterotto, J.G. (1995). A framework for assessment in multicultural counseling. In J.G. Ponterotto, J.M. Casas, L.A. Suzuki, & C.M. Alexander (Eds.), *Handbook of multicultural counseling* (pp. 357-374). London: Sage.

Gudykunst, W. B., & Nishida, T. (2001). Anxiety, uncertainty, and perceived effectiveness of communication across relationships and cultures. *International Journal of Intercultural Relations, 25*, 55-71.

Gullahorn, J., & Gullahorn, J. (1963). An extension of the U-curve hypothesis. *Social Issues, 19*, 33-47.

Guthrie, G.M. (1975). A behavioral analysis of culture learning. In R.W. Brislin, S. Bochner, W.J. Lonner (Eds.), *Cross-cultural perspectives on learning* (pp. 95-116). New York: John Wiley and Sons.

Hammer, M. R. (1992). Research, mission statements, and international student advising offices. *International Journal of Intercultural Relations, 16*, 217-236.

Han, G.S., Jamieson, M. I., & Young, A. E. (2000). Schooling in rural New South Wales: The experience of overseas Students. *Journal of Family Studies, 6*(2), 272-279.

Harrison, J.K., Chadwick, M., & Scales, M. (1996). The relationship between cross-cultural adjustment and the personality variables of self-efficacy and self-monitoring. *International Journal of Intercultural Relations, 20*, 167-188.

Hayes, R.L., & Lin, H. (1994). Coming to America: Developing social support systems for international students. *Journal of Multicultural Counseling and Development, 22*, 7-16.

Helms, J.E. (1986). Expanding racial identity theory to cover counseling process. *Journal of Counseling Psychology, 33*, 62-64.

Helms, J.E. (1994). How multiculturalism obscures racial factors in the therapy process: Comment on Ridley et al. (1994), Sodowsky et al. (1994), Ottavi et al. (1994), and Thompson et al. (1994). *Journal of Counseling Psychology, 41*, 162-165.

Helms, J.E. (1995). An update of Helm's White and People of Color racial identity models. In J.G. Ponterotto, J.M. Casas, L.A. Suzuki, & C.M. Alexander (Eds.), *Handbook of multicultural counseling* (pp. 181-198). London: Sage.

Heppner, M.J., & O'Brien, K.M. (1994). Multi-cultural counselor training: An examination of students' perceptions of helpful and hindering events. *Counselor Education and Supervision, 34*, 4-18.

Ho, D. Y. F. (1995). Internalized culture, culturocentrism, and transcendence. *The Counseling Psychologist, 23*(1), 4-24.

Holmes, J. (1996). Export-readiness in the Canadian education sector. *CBIE Research, 8*, 1-15. Humphries, J. (1996/97). *The national report of international students in Canada 1996/97*. Ottawa, ON: Canadian Bureau for International Education.

Huxur, G., Mansfield, E., Nnazor, R., Schuetze, H., & Segawa, M. (1996).

Learning needs and adaptation problems of foreign graduate students. *Canadian Society for the Study of Higher Education, 15*, 1-16.

Ishiyama, F.I. (1989). Understanding foreign adolescents' difficulties in cross-cultural adjustment: A self-validation model. *Canadian Journal of School Psychology, 5*(1), 41-56.

Ishiyama, F.I. (1995a). Use of validationgram in counseling: Exploring sources of self-validation and impact in personal transition. *Canadian Journal of Counseling, 29*, 134-146.

Ishiyama, F.I. (1995b). Culturally dislocated clients: Self-validation and cultural conflict issues and counseling implications. *Canadian Journal of Counseling, 29*, 262-275.

Jacob, E. J., & Greggo, J. W. (2001). Using counselor training and collaborative programming strategies in working with international students. *Journal of Multicultural Counseling and Development, 29*, 73-88.

Jochems, W., Snippe, J., Smid, H.J., & Verweij, A. (1996). The academic progress of foreign students: Study achievement and study behavior. *Higher Education, 31*, 325-340.

Johnston, J., & Edelstein, R. (1993). *Beyond borders.* Washington, DC: Association of American Colleges.

Kamal, A.A., & Maruyama, G. (1990). Cross-cultural contact and attitudes of Qatari students in the United States. *International Journal of Intercultural Relations, 14*, 123-134.

Kane, M., & Humphries, J. (1999). *The national report of international students in Canada 1998/99.* Ottawa, ON: Canadian Bureau for International Education.

Kim, Y. (1991). Intercultural communication competence: A systems-theoretic view. In S. Ting-Toomey & F. Korzenny (Eds.), *Cross-cultural interpersonal communication* (pp. 259-275). Newbury Park: Sage.

Knight, J. (1994). Internationalization: Elements and checkpoints. *CBIE Research, 7*, 1-15. Knight, J. (1999). A time of turbulence and transformation for internationalization. *CBIE Research, 14*, 1-19.

Knight, J. (2000). *Progress & promise: The AUCC report on internationalization at Canadian universities.* Ottawa, ON: Association of Universities and Colleges of Canada.

Knight, J. (2001). Monitoring the quality and progress of internationalization. *Journal of Studies in International Education, 5*(3), 228-243.

Kwan, K.L. K., Sodowsky, G. R., & Ihle, G. M. (1994). Worldviews of Chinese international students: An extension and new findings. *Journal of College Student Development, 35*, 190-197.

LaBrack, B. (1993). The missing linkage: The process of integrating orientation and reentry. In R.M. Paige (Ed.), *Education for the intercultural experience* (pp. 241-280). Yarmouth, ME: Intercultural Press.

LaFromboise, T. D., Foster, S., & James, A. (1996). Ethics in multicultural counseling. In P. B. Pedersen & J. G. Draguns & W. J. Lonner & J. E. Trimble (Eds.), *Counseling Across Cultures* (4th ed.) (pp. 47-72). Thousand Oaks, CA: Sage.

Lambert, R.D. (1992). *Foreign student flows and the internationalization of higher education: NAFSA Working Paper #37.* Evans City, PA: NAFSA Publications.

Lazarus, R. (1993). From psychological stress to the emotions: A history of changing outlooks. *Annual Review of Psychology, 44,* 1-21.

Lazarus, R.S. (1997). Acculturation isn't everything. *Applied Psychology: An International Review, 46,* 39-43.

Lazarus, R., & Folkman, S. (1984). *Stress, appraisal, and coping.* New York: Springer.

Leberman, K. (1994). Asian student perspectives on American university instruction. *International Journal of Intercultural Relations, 18,* 173-192.

Lecca, P.J., Quervalu, I., Nunes, J.V., & Gonzales, H.F. (1998). *Cultural competency in health, social & human services: Directions for the twenty-first century.* New York, NT: Garland Publishing, Inc.

Lee, D. S. (1997). What teachers can do to relieve problems identified by international students. *New Directions for Teaching and Learning, 70,* 93-100.

Lee, F.Y. (1991). *The relationship of ethnic identity to social support, self-esteem, psychological distress, and help-seeking behavior among Asian American college students.* Unpublished doctoral dissertation, University of Illinois, Urbana-Champaign.

Leong, F. T., & Chou, E. L. (1996). Counseling International Students. In P. B. Pedersen & J. G. Draguns & W. J. Lonner & J. E. Trimble (Eds.), *Counseling Across Cultures* (4th ed.) (pp. 210-242). Thousand Oaks, CA: Sage.

Leong, F.T., & Sedlacek, W.E. (1986). A comparison of international and U.S. student preferences for help sources. *Journal of College Student Personnel, 27,* 426-430.

Leung, S.A. (1995). Career development and counseling: A multicultural perspective. In J.G. Ponterotto, J.M. Casas, L.A. Suzuki, & C.M. Alexander (Eds.), *Handbook of multicultural counseling* (pp. 549-566). Thousand Oaks, CA: Sage.

Liberman, K. (1994). Asian student perspectives on American university instruction. *International Journal of Intercultural Relations, 18*(2), 173-192.

Lin, J.C. G., & Yi, J. K. (1997). Asian international students' adjustment: Issues and program suggestions. *College Student Journal, 31*, 473-479.

Luk, B. (1997). Canadian education, Asia Pacific relations, and Asian student mobility. In J. Humphries (Ed.), *The national report on international students in Canada 1996/97* (pp. 42-50). Ottawa, ON: Canadian Bureau for International Education.

Luzzo, D.A., Henao, C., & Wilson, M. (1996). An innovative approach to assessing the academic and social needs of international students. *Journal of College Student Development, 37*, 351-352.

Lysgaard, S. (1955). Adjustment in a foreign society: Norwegian Fulbright grantees visiting the United States. *International Social Science Bulletin, 10*, 45-51.

Mallinckrodt, B., & Leong, F.T. (1992). International graduate students, stress, and social support. *Journal of College Student Development, 33*, 71-78.

Marginson, S. (1997). *Markets in education.* St. Leonard's, Australia: Allen and Unwin.

Martin, J.N. (1984). The intercultural reentry: Conceptualization and directions for future research. *International Journal of Intercultural Relations, 8*, 115-134.

Martin, J.N., & Harrell, T. (1996). Reentry training for intercultural sojourners. In D. Landis & R.S. Bhagat (Eds.). *Handbook of intercultural training* (2nd ed.) (pp. 307-326). Thousand Oaks, CA: Sage.

Matsui, M. (1988). Comparative study of female overseas students from Japan and the People's Republic of China at an American university. *Educational Resources Information Center (ERIC)*, 1-45.

May, W.C., & Jepsen, D.A. (1988). Attitudes toward counselors and counseling process: A comparison of Chinese and American graduate students. *Journal of Counseling and Development, 67*, 189-192.

McIntosh, P. (1988). *White privilege and male privilege: A personal account of coming to see correspondences through work in women's studies* (Working Papers Series No. 189). Wellesley, MA: Wellesley College, Center for Research on Women.

McIntosh, P. (1998). White privilege: unpacking the invisible knapsack. In M. McGoldrick (Ed.), *Re-visioning family therapy: Race, culture and gender in clinical practice* (pp. 147-152). New York: Guilford.

McKinlay, H.J, Pattison, H.M., & Gross, H. (1996). An exploratory investigation of the effects of a cultural orientation programme on the psychological well-being of international university students. *Higher Education, 31*, 379-395.

McLennan, N., Rochow, S., & Arthur, N. (2001). Religious and spiritual diversity in counseling. *Guidance and Counseling, 16*, 132-137.

Mori, S. (2000). Addressing the mental health concerns of international students. *Journal of Counseling & Development, 78*, 137-144.

NAFSA: Association of International Educators (1992). *Code of ethics.* Sewickley, PA: Author.

NAFSA: Association of International Educators (1996). *NAFSA's international student handbook.* Washington, DC: Author.

Nesdale, D., & Todd, P. (2000). Effect of contact on intercultural acceptance: a field study. *International Journal of Intercultural Relations, 24, 341-360.*

Neville, H.A., Worthington, R.L., & Spanierman, L.B. (2001). Race, power, and multicultural counseling psychology: understanding white privilege and color-blind racial attitudes. In J.G. Ponterotto, J.M. Casas, L.A. Suzuki, L.A., & C.M. Alexander (Eds.), *Handbook of multicultural counseling* (2nd ed.) (pp. 257-288). Thousand Oaks, CA: Sage.

North, D.M. (2002). U.S. must balance pilot training and security. *Aviation Week & Space Technology, 156*(24), 1-2.

Oberg, K. (1960). Cultural shock: Adjustment to new cultural environments. *Practical Anthropology, 7*, 177-182.

Paniagua, F. A. (2001). *Diagnosis in a multicultural context: A casebook for mental health professionals.* Thousand Oaks, CA: Sage.

Parker, B., & McEvoy, G.M. (1993). Initial examination of a model of intercultural adjustment. *International Journal of Intercultural Relations, 17*, 355-379.

Parr, G., Bradley, L., & Bingi, R. (1992). Concerns and feelings of international students. *Journal of College Student Development, 33*, 20-25.

Pedersen, P. (1988). *A handbook for developing multicultural awareness.* Washington, DC: American Association for Counseling and Development.

Pedersen, P. (1990). Social and psychological factors of brain drain and reentry among international students: A survey of this topic. *McGill Journal of Education, 25*, 229-243.

Pedersen, P. (1991). Counseling international students. *The Counseling Psychologist, 19*, 10-58.

Pedersen, P. (1995a). *The five stages of culture shock.* Westport, CN: Greenwood Press.

Pedersen, P. (1995b). The culture-bound counselor as an unintentional racist. *Canadian Journal of Counseling, 29,* 197-205.

Pedersen, P. (1995c). Culture-centered ethical guidelines for counsellors. In J.G. Ponterotto, J.M. Casas, L.A. Suzuki, L.A., & C.M. Alexander (Eds.), *Handbook of multicultural counseling* (1st ed.) (pp. 34-50). Thousand Oaks, CA: Sage.

Pedersen, P. (1997). The cultural context of the American counseling association of ethics. *Journal of Counseling & Development, 76,* 23-28.

Pedersen, P. (2001). Multiculturalism and the paradigm shift in counseling: Controversies and alternative futures. *Canadian Journal of Counseling, 35,* 15-25.

Pedersen, P., & Ivey, A. (1993). *Culture-centered counseling and interviewing skills: A practical guide.* Westport, CT: Praeger.

Petress, K. C. (1995). Coping with a new educational environment: Chinese students' imagined interactions before commencing studies in the U.S. *Journal of Instructional Psychology, 22*(1), 50-63.

Pettifor, J. (2001). Are professional codes of ethics relevant for multicultural counseling? *Canadian Journal of Counseling, 35,* 26-35.

Ponterotto, J.G., Casas, J.M., Suzuki, L.A., & Alexander, C.M. (Eds.). (1995). *Handbook of multicultural counseling.* Thousand Oaks, CA: Sage.

Ponterotto, J.G., Casas, J.M., Suzuki, L.A., & Alexander, C.M. (Eds.). (2001). *Handbook of multicultural counseling* (2nd ed.). Thousand Oaks, CA: Sage.

Popadiuk, N., & Arthur, N. (in press). Counseling international students in Canadian schools. *International Journal for the Advancement of Counseling.*

Raschio, R.A. (1987). College students' perceptions of reverse culture shock and reentry adjustments. *Journal of College Student Personnel, 28,* 156-162.

Redmond, M.V. (2000). Cultural distance as a mediating factor between stress and intercultural communication competence. *International Journal of Intercultural Relations,* 24, 151-159.

Redmond, M.V., & Bunyi, J.M. (1993). The relationship of intercultural communication competence with stress and the handling of stress as reported by international students. *International Journal of Intercultural Relations, 17,* 235-254.

Ridley, C.R. (1995). *Overcoming unintentional racism in counseling and therapy: A practitioner's guide to intentional intervention.* Thousand Oaks: Sage.

Ridley, C. R., Li, L. C., & Hill, C. L. (1998). Multicultural assessment: Reexamination, reconceptualization, and practical application. *The Counseling Psychologist, 26,* 827-910.

Ridley, C.R., Liddle, M.C., Hill, C.L., & Li, L.C. (2001). Ethical decision making in multicultural counseling. In J.G. Ponterotto, J.M. Casas, L.A. Suzuki, L.A., & C.M. Alexander (Eds.), *Handbook of multicultural counseling* (2nd ed.) (pp. 165-188). Thousand Oaks, CA: Sage.

Ridley, C.R., & Lingle, D.W. (1996). Cultural empathy in multicultural counseling: A multidimensional process model. In P.B. Pedersen, J.G. Draguns, W.J. Lonner, & J.E. Trimble (Eds.), *Counseling across cultures* (4th ed.), (pp. 21-46). Thousand Oaks, CA: Sage.

Ridley, C.R., Mendoza, D.W., Kanitz, B.E., Angermeier, L., & Zenk, R. (1994). Cultural sensitivity in multicultural counseling: A perceptual schema model. *Journal of Counseling Psychology, 41, 125-136.*

Rogers, J. & Ward, C. (1993). Expectation-experience discrepancies and psychological adjustment during cross-cultural reentry. *International Journal of Intercultural Relations, 17,* 185-196.

Rowe, W., Bennett, S., & Atkinson, D.R. (1994). White racial identity models: A critique and alternative proposal. *Counseling Psychologist, 22,* 120-146.

Ruiz, A.S. (1990). Ethnic identity: Crisis and resolution. *Journal of Multicultural Counseling and Development, 18,* 29-40.

Ryan, M.E., & Twibell, R.S. (2000). Concerns, values, stress, coping, health and educational outcomes of college students who studied abroad. *International Journal of Intercultural Relations, 24,* 409-435.

Saidla, D.D., & Grant, S. (1993). Roommate understanding and rapport between international and American roommates. *Journal of College Student Development, 34,* 335-340.

Sandhu, D.S. (1994). An examination of the psychological needs of students: Implications for counseling and psychotherapy. *International Journal for the Advancement of Counseling, 17,* 229-239.

Sandhu, D.S., & Asrabadi, B.R. (1994). Development of an acculturative stress scale for international students: Preliminary findings. *Psychological Reports, 75,* 435-448.

Schlossberg, N. (1984). *Counseling adults in transition: Linking practice with theory.* New York: Springer.

Schlossberg, N. (1992). Adult development theories: Ways to illuminate the adult development experience. In H.D. Lea & Z.B. Leibowitz (Eds.), *Adult career development: Concepts, issues, and practices* (2nd Ed.), (pp. 2-16). Alexandria, VA: The National Career Development Association.

Searle, W., & Ward, C. (1990). The prediction of psychological and sociocultural adjustment during cross-cultural transitions. *International Journal of Intercultural Relations, 14*, 449-464.

Sheehan, O.T. & Pearson, F. (1995). Asian international and American students' psychosocial development. *Journal of College Student Development, 36*(6), 522-530.

Shih, S., & Brown, C. (2000). Taiwanese international students: acculturation level and vocational identity. *Journal of Career Development, 27*(1), 35-47.

Shougee, M. (1999). *The experiences, meanings and outcomes of studying abroad: A qualitative multiple-case study.* Unpublished Ph.D. dissertation, University of Toronto, Toronto.

Siegel, C. (1991). Counseling international students: A clinician's comments. *The Counseling Psychologist, 19*, 72-75.

Singelis, T.M., & Pedersen, P. (1997). Conflict and mediation across cultures. In K. Cushner & R.W. Brislin (Eds.), *Improving intercultural interactions: Modules for cross-cultural training programs, Volume 2* (pp. 184-204). Thousand Oaks, CA: Sage.

Sodowsky, G.R., & Plake, B.S. (1992). A study of acculturation differences among international people and suggestions for sensitivity to within-group differences. *Journal of Counseling & Development, 71,* 53-59.

Sodowsky, G. R., & Plake, B. S. (1992). A study of acculturation differences among international people and suggestions for sensitivity to within-group differences. *Journal of Counseling & Development, 71,* 53-59.

Smalley, W.A. (1963). Culture shock, language shock, and the shock of self-discovery. *Practical Anthropology, 10*, 49-56.

Spencer-Rodgers. (2000). The vocational situation and country of orientation of international students. *Journal of Multicultural Counseling and Development, 28,* 32-49.

Stewart, J. (2000). Using the culture grid in culture-centered assessment. *Guidance & Counselling, 18* (1), 10-17.

Sue, D.W., Arrendondo, P., & McDavis, R. (1992). Multicultural counseling competencies and standards: A call to the profession. *Journal of Counseling and Development, 70,* 477-486.

Sue, D.W., Bernier, J.B., Durran, M., Feinberg, L., Pederse, P., Smith, E., Vasquez-Nuttall, E. (1982). Position paper: Cross-cultural counseling competencies. *Counseling Psychologist, 10,* 45-52.

Sue, D.W., Carter, R.T., Casa, J.M., Fouad, N.A., Ivey, A.E., Jensen, M., LaFromboise, T., Manese, J.E., Ponterotto, J.G., & Vazquez-Nutall, E. (1998). *Multicultural counseling competencies: Individual and organizational development.* Thousand Oaks, CA: Sage.

Sue, D.W., Ivey, A.E., & Pedersen, P.B. (1996). *A theory of multicultural counseling and therapy.* Pacific Grove, CA: Brooks/Cole.

Sue, D. W., & Sue, D. (1990). *Counseling the culturally-different: Theory and practice (2nd ed.).* New York: Wiley & Sons.

Sue, D. W., & Sue, D. (1999). *Counseling the culturally-different: Theory and practice (3rd ed.).* New York: Wiley & Sons.

Sue, D., & Sundberg, N. D. (1996). Research and research hypotheses about effectiveness in intercultural counseling. In P. B. Pedersen, J. G. Draguns, W. J. Lonner, & J. E. Trimble (Eds.), *Counseling across cultures* (4th ed.) (pp. 323-352). Thousand Oaks, CA: Sage.

Sue, S., & Sue, D.W. (1971). Chinese American personality and mental health. *Amerasian Journal, 1,* 36-49.

Sussman, N.M. (2000). The dynamic nature of cultural identity throughout cultural transitions: why home is not so sweet. *Personality and Social Psychological Review, 4,* 355-373.

Tanaka, T., Takai, J., Kohyama, T., Fuhihara, T., & Minami, H. (1997). Effects of social networks on cross-cultural adjustment. *Japanese Psychological Research, 39* (1), 12-24.

Tanaka, T., Takai. J., Takaya, K., & Fujihara, T. (1994). Adjustment patterns of international students in Japan. *International Journal of Intercultural Relations, 18,* 55-75.

Tanaka-Matsumi, J., & Higginbotham, H. N. (1996). Behavioral approaches to counseling across cultures. In P. B. Pedersen, J. G. Draguns, W. J. Lonner, & J. E. Trimble (Eds.), *Counseling across cultures* (4th ed.) (pp. 266-292). Thousand Oaks, CA: Sage.

Tapper, J. (1996). Exchange patterns in the oral discourse of international students in university classrooms. *Discourse Processes, 22,* 25-55.

Thomas, K., & Althen, G. (1989). Counseling foreign students. In P.B. Pedersen, J.G., Draguns, W.J. Lonner, & J.E. Trimble (Eds.), *Counseling across cultures* (3rd ed.) (pp. 205-241). Honolulu: University of Hawaii Press.

The Australian Government International Education Network. (2003). *Overseas student statistics 2000 – summary of key points.* Retrieved April 7, 2003, from http://www.aei.dest.gov.au/general/stats/OSS2k/ OSS2k.htm

Tillman, M.J. (1990). Effective support services for international students. *New Directions For Community Colleges, 70,* 87-98.

Triandis, H.C. (1991). A need for theoretical examination. *The Counseling Psychologist, 19,* 59-61.

Tyler, A., & Boxer, D. (1996). Sexual harassment? Cross-cultural/cross-linguistic perspectives. *Discourse Society, 7*(1), 107-133.

Uehara, A. (1986). The nature of American student reentry adjustment and perceptions of the sojourn experience. *International Journal of Intercultural Relations, 10*, 415-438.

Volet, S.E., & Renshaw, P.D. (1995). Cross-cultural differences in university students' goals and perceptions of study settings for achieving their own goals. *Higher Education, 30*, 407-433.

Walker, J. L. (1999). *Canada first: The 1999 survey of international students.* Ottawa, ON: Canadian Bureau for International Education.

Walton, S.J. (1990). Stress management training for overseas effectiveness. *International Journal of Intercultural Relations, 14*, 507-527.

Wan, T., Chapman, D.W., & Biggs, D.A. (1992). Academic stress of international students attending U.S. Universities. *Research in Higher Education, 33*, 607-623.

Wang, M.M. (1997). Reentry and reverse culture shock. In K. Cushner & R.W. Brislin (Eds.), *Improving intercultural interactions: Modules for cross-cultural training programs, Volume 2* (pp. 109-128). Thousand Oaks, CA: Sage.

Ward, C., Bochner, S., & Furnam, A. (2001). *The psychology of culture shock* (2nd ed.). East Sussex: Routledge.

Ward, C., & Kennedy, A. (1993). Where's the "culture" in cross-cultural transition? Comparative studies of sojourner adjustment. *Journal of Cross-Cultural Psychology, 24*, 221-249.

Warner, G. (1992). Internationalization models and the role of the university. *CBIE International Education Magazine*, p.21.

Weeks, W.H., Pedersen, P.B., & Brislin, R.W. (1979). *A manual of structured experiences for cross-cultural learning.* Yarmouth, ME: Intercultural Press.

Wehrly, B. (1988). Cultural diversity from an international perspective, part 2. *Journal of Multicultural Counseling and Development, 16*(1), 3-15.

Weinrach, S.G., & Thomas, K.R. (1996). The counseling profession's commitment to diversity-sensitive counseling: A critical reassessment. *Journal of Counseling and Development, 74*, 472-477.

Westwood, M.J., Lawrence, W.S., & Paul, D. (1986). Preparing for reentry: A program for the sojourning student. *International Journal for the Advancement of Counseling, 9*, 221-230.

Westwood, M.J., & Barker, M. (1990). Academic achievement and social adaptation among international students: A comparison groups study of the peer-pairing program. *International Journal of Intercultural Relations, 14*, 251-263.

Westwood, M.J., Lawrence, W.S., & Paul, D. (1986). Preparing for re-entry: A program for the sojourning student. *International Journal for the Advancement of Counseling, 9*, 221-230.

Wilson, B.G. (1991). *The impact of export development on the domestic education market.* Exporting Education: AIC Conference, Australia.

Winkelman, M. (1994). Cultural shock and adaptation. *Journal of Counseling and Development, 73,* 121-126.

Wong-Rieger, D. (1984). Testing a model of emotional and coping responses to problems in adaptation: Foreign students at a Canadian university. *International Journal of Intercultural Relations, 8,* 153-184.

Wrenn, C.G. (1962). The culturally encapsulated counselor. *Harvard Educational Review, 32,* 444-449.

Yang, B., Teraoka, M., Eichenfield, G. A., & Audas, M. C. (1994). Meaningful relationships between Asian international and U.S. college students: A descriptive study. *College Student Journal,* 108-115.

Yau, T.Y., Sue, D., & Hayden, D. (1992). Counseling style preference of international students. *Journal of Counseling Psychology, 39, 100-104.*

Ying, Y.W., & Liese, L.H. (1990). Initial adaptation of Taiwan foreign students to the United States: The impact of prearrival variables. *American Journal of Community Psychology, 18*(6), 825-845.

Zaharna, R.S. (1989). Self-shock: The double-binding challenge of identity. *International Journal of Intercultural Relations, 13,* 501-525.

Zhang, D. (1995). Depression and culture - a Chinese perspective. *Canadian Journal of Counseling, 29,* 227-233.

Zhang, N. (1998). *Acculturation and counseling expectancies: Asian international students' attitudes toward seeking professional psychological help.* Unpublished Ph.D. Dissertation, Ball State University, Muncie, Indiana.

Zimmermann, S. (1995). Perceptions of intercultural communication competence and international student adaptation to an American campus. *Communication Education, 44,* 321-33

Index

148 COUNSELING INTERNATIONAL STUDENTS

Breinigsville, PA USA
02 March 2010
233293BV00006B/2/P